S0-BZL-050

TERROR OF DEMONS

TERROR
— OF —
DEMONS

RECLAIMING
TRADITIONAL
CATHOLIC
MASCULINITY

KENNEDY HALL

TAN Books
Gastonia, North Carolina

Terror of Demons: Reclaiming Traditional Catholic Masculinity © 2021 Kennedy Hall

All rights reserved. With the exception of short excerpts used in critical review, no part of this work may be reproduced, transmitted, or stored in any form whatsoever, without the prior written permission of the publisher. Creation, exploitation and distribution of any unauthorized editions of this work, in any format in existence now or in the future—including but not limited to text, audio, and video—is prohibited without the prior written permission of the publisher.

Scripture quotations are from the Douay-Rheims 1899 American Edition.

Cover design by Caroline Green

Cover images: The Nativity (detail of St. Joseph), 1639 (oil on copper), Stella, Jacques (1596-1657), © Bowes Museum / Bridgeman Images. Allegory of the Suppression of the German Revolution (detail of demon), 1848-49, German School, (19th century), © Deutsches Historisches Museum / © DHM / Bridgeman Images. Clouds opening up to Heaven, digital illustration by Amanda Carden/Shutterstock.

Library of Congress Control Number: 2021946768

ISBN: 978-1-5051-2254-1
Kindle ISBN: 978-1-5051-2255-8
ePUB ISBN: 978-1-5051-2256-5

Published in the United States by
TAN Books
PO Box 269
Gastonia, NC 28053
www.TANBooks.com

Printed in the United States of America

CONTENTS

PROTESTATION

IN all that I shall say in this book, I submit to what is taught by our mother, the Holy Roman Church; if there is anything in it contrary to this, it will be without my knowledge. Therefore, for the love of Our Lord, I beg the learned men who read this book to look at it very carefully and make known to me any faults of this nature, and any other kinds of errors, which may be in it. If there is anything good in it, let this be to the glory and honor of God in the service of his most sacred Mother, our Patroness and Lady.[1]

KENNEDY HALL

---

1   Adapted from the protestation given by St. Teresa of Avila in *The Way of Perfection*.

PREFACE

"Undertake this journey eagerly for the remission of your sins, with the assurance of the reward of imperishable glory in the kingdom of heaven."

—Blessed Pope Urban II

I wrote this book because Catholic men need a book like this. I also wrote this book as a spiritual exercise for myself. Every day, I seek to be a better and manlier Catholic, so I thought I should put this in print. The content of this book is challenging, and I continue to be challenged by it. There is a host of useful books to read on every aspect of the spiritual and moral life, but, to my mind, it is hard to find a resource that is a one-stop shop for men who want to develop heroic virtue. I have a book in my bedside table drawer called *The DIY Bible*. The book explains how to fix most issues that come up in the realm of home improvement and maintenance. There is the odd job that requires a specialist who is highly trained, but in reading through that book, I realized I could fix most things if I put in the work. In a similar manner, this book will act as a guide for most things that pertain to Catholic masculinity.

If taken seriously, this book will help you grow in virtue and seek true Catholic masculinity. For some, this will mean a radical change in lifestyle; for others, it will mean using this book as something to reignite a fire to go from good to excellent. You will be equipped to identify the demands of true manliness and utilize strategies to fight. You will equip yourself to work alongside St. Michael and watch him *cast into hell Satan and all evil spirits who wander around the earth seeking the ruin of souls.*

Before you begin reading, it is necessary to understand something: *the devil will not like you reading this book, and he will come after you.* Even in the writing process, I encountered constant resistance. This book will help you go from the highway to hell to the narrow path. If you are already on the narrow path, it will help you supercharge your steps on the stairway to heaven. The devil hates virtue, he hates losing souls to God, and he wants to keep you in a state of mortal sin or spiritual complacency. Once he realizes that you are kicking things into high gear, he will throw many tantrums, and so will his legions. Prepare yourself and please say a Hail Mary for the author.

Because of this impending attack, you need to make three fundamental commitments as a baseline:

1. Make the Rosary a daily habit. Maybe you already pray the Rosary daily; this is good. If you don't, you have to start. It takes about fifteen to twenty minutes to pray a five-decade Rosary. Split it up into chunks if you have to, or simply skip watching another rerun of a sitcom or stop wasting your time watching the news. Our Lady has appeared multiple times over the past few centuries, and she has always insisted on praying the Rosary. If you aren't going to commit to the Rosary, then you aren't serious about salvation.

2. Get all the evil images out of your life.[1] This means
   all of the evil images. Of course, it is easy to identify the explicitly evil, pornographic material, but
   all sexually suggestive material must go. If you are
   addicted to evil images, you may literally have to
   destroy your phone and throw away your computer.
   Isn't that a little bit extreme? Am I really supposed
   to throw out an expensive piece of technology just
   because I can use it to watch evil images? Yes!
   First, this remedy will be temporary until you get
   a handle on things, and secondly, you may need to
   make a choice: throw away the tech or throw away
   your soul. We will go into more detail later in the
   book on how to make your home safe from evil
   images, but for now, if you have an issue, take drastic and surgical steps. If you watch evil images on
   your phone or computer today and then slip in the
   shower and break your neck and die before confessing, you will be damned. This should be fright-
   ening. Time to be scared straight.

3. Make a good examination of conscience and go to
   confession as soon as possible. You need to be sure
   that you have confessed all your known mortal sins
   in order to live in a state of grace. If you aren't living in a state of grace, then your intellect is darkened and you will be more susceptible to demonic influence as you read this book. If you are in a

---

1 Throughout this book, the phrase "evil images" will be used solely
   to describe the evil of pornography; though evil images can also
   include impure thoughts, memories, and phantasms (picture-
   thoughts of the imagination).

state of mortal sin, you are weak, and when you are weak, you are soft; when you are soft, you cease to be a man. Do not be soft. Get to confession and make sure you are cleaned up.

Online Resources

Throughout the book, the reader will notice that at times he will be instructed to visit a website. To access these resources, go to meaningofcatholic.com/terrorofdemons. Here you will find a host of helpful resources that help to implement the contents of the book into daily life.

ACKNOWLEDGMENTS

TO my wife. I owe you more than I can say. Without you, I would not be the man I am. Because of you and the children whom you have given me, fighting against the culture is a daily joy. Every man needs a woman to fight for; I could not ask for one better. If I were to write down all my thoughts, "the world itself, I think, would not be able to contain the books that should be written" (Jn. 21:25). One lifetime is not enough.

To Nonno, Giuseppe Viani. God rest your soul. If I become half the man you were, I will be twice the man I am now. We all stand on the shoulders of giants, and I stand on the strongest. Thank you for giving me a heritage in faith worth fighting for.

Finally, to glorious St. Joseph. Like in Scripture, there is scant mention of your name in this book, but your perfected virtue and masculinity is woven into every page. St. Joseph, Terror of Demons, pray for us!

KENNEDY HALL
St. Joseph the Worker
Anno Domini MMXX

INTRODUCTION

YEARS ago, I sat in a pew at St. Peter's Cathedral Basilica in my hometown of London, Ontario. I looked over at three men whom I respected very much as they knelt in prayer before Mass. It was an 8:30 a.m. Mass, a Sunday, and also the morning of a very important football game for us at Catholic Central High School (CCH). We had a tradition at CCH wherein we attended Mass the morning of every game throughout the season. We never played on Sundays, but it was the Ontario Western Bowl semi-final, and the game scheduled for the previous day had been snowed-out. It was the first week of December, and this is what happens in the southwestern Ontario snow-belt. We were playing on artificial turf, so a snowplow was used to clear off the field in order for us to play the game. For any Americans reading this, you should imagine the most stereotypical scene of Canadian football, as we played football in sub-zero weather with sidelines marked by walls of snow. It was an incredible game. We won, and the following week, we went on to win a Western Bowl championship at a much warmer indoor venue in Toronto.

What does this story about high school football have to do with Catholic masculinity? Well, I am more concerned with the three men I saw kneeling at Mass than I am with the game. You see, these were our three coaches—our head coach and two assistants. These three men were giants to me not only because they were physically imposing football coaches but also because they were true leaders. They commanded my respect, and I would have done anything they asked. These men were Roman Catholic men.

I didn't grow up in a family that practiced the Faith. In fact, I barely remember going to Easter or Christmas Mass as a child, except perhaps with my Nonno and Nonna. May God rest their souls. My mother is an Italian immigrant, and my father descends from English Catholics. In typical post-Vatican II fashion, the older generation was pious, and the boomer generation had more or less given up on the Faith a long time ago. My mother has kept the Faith to a degree, and I pray for her to become a consistent, practicing Catholic. My father, who was a Latin Mass altar-server for his whole life until the 1970 "wreckovation" of the Mass, comes to church when our children receive sacraments. I love my father, and I pray he will find his way home so we can spend eternity together. In fact, I have joked with him that my wife and I seem to have a new child every year because it means he has to step into a church at least annually for a baptism.

In any case, I grew up with nothing more than a vague cultural Catholicism and a less than ideal Catholic education. In fact, my "education" was so feeble that I distinctly remember a religion teacher in grade ten saying that we should "not think of the Holy Bible as true necessarily but as a book with really good messages." That's right, a secondary school religion teacher told his students that the Holy Bible shouldn't be thought of as "true."

Despite the lack of religious formation and the fact that I was leading a relatively sinful life, the image of those men kneeling in prayer was somehow still etched into my brain. In my early twenties, while applying to Teachers College, the memory of these men kneeling in prayer was invaluable in my reconsideration of the Faith. At any rate, at this time I was essentially a lapsed Catholic and a secular humanist. I was not an atheist in the truest sense of the word, even though I tried to be, God forgive me. Like many men, I held that Catholicism was superstitious and out of touch with the modern world. I believed I was so much smarter than people who were fooled by religion. I was arrogant, and although I was academic, I was foolish. Despite my arrogance, in spite of my foolishness, I knew there was something to Catholicism, something that pulled on my heartstrings. I couldn't bring myself to believe that I was above these men who believed the Faith and who had done so much for me. Cutting through the fog of my pretentious worldview was a sliver of integrity. I had many vices, and I was not living in a state of grace. I was not on my way to heaven, but somehow I still believed in some vague notion of history and tradition. I knew that gratitude had to be extended to my ancestors and that somewhere deep down I wasn't as smart as I thought I was. I owed it to those three coaches and others to give the faith a second look. I wanted to be a high school teacher, I wanted to coach. In essence, I wanted to be like them. I couldn't bring myself to believe that these men were somehow foolish. The memory of these three men on their *knees* made them stand *tall* in my mind.

My conversion was at times slow, and at other times lightning fast, as these things tend to be. Years later, I now find myself a Rosary-praying, Latin Mass-attending Catholic father of four who hopes to share the Faith that saved his soul. It is a mystery to me how I arrived here, and I guess I will see all the dots connected when, God willing, I share in the Beatific Vision. Until then, I cannot ignore the fire in my soul that compels me to do all I can to inspire other men to embrace the Catholic faith.

Our culture is effeminate, our men are soft, and our souls are being cast into hell at an alarming rate. Men spend more time staring at evil images on their phone than they do staring at the cross or an icon of the Most Blessed Virgin. Men are weaker than they have ever been, and our civilization is perishing before our very eyes as a result. We have given into feminism, religious indifferentism, scientism, and paganism. We defer to every other "ism" besides the only true "ism," Catholicism. The highway to hell is an eight-lane expressway at this point, and it is time for men to wake up and smell the sulfur. "For wide is the gate, and broad is the way that leadeth to destruction, and many there are who go in thereat" (Mt. 7:13). This saying of Jesus Christ could be the motto of our society and is the best descriptor of the plight of men today. We are gallivanting down the wide path; we are walking off a cliff into the depths of eternal hellfire. We do not even realize it because we won't stop to look up from the evil images on our iPhones. Our Lord told us that many will walk the path to destruction. It is not a matter of whether some men will go to hell but rather *how many*. Do you know where you are headed? We dare not hope that all men will achieve salvation, and we dare not count ourselves as part of the saved if we continue to live as we are. It has long been the time for men to wake up, stand up, grow up, and man up. We need more than mere men; we need *traditional Catholic men*.

1

THE DEVIL IS REAL AND HE WANTS YOUR SOUL

"Not all, nor even a majority, are saved. . . . They are indeed many, if regarded by themselves, but they are few in comparison with the far larger number of those who shall be punished with the devil."

—St. Augustine

"The Devil is like a mad dog tied by a chain. Beyond the length of the chain he cannot catch hold of anyone. And you, therefore, keep your distance. If you get too close you will be caught. Remember, the Devil has only one door with which to enter into our soul: our will."

—St. Padre Pio

IF you were to ask your average Catholic about the reality of the devil, sadly I would imagine that many would scoff at the idea. Surveys show that most baptized Catholics do not believe in the infernal dragon and his henchmen.[1] Even weekly Mass attendees have grown soft in their belief about the enemy. Sure, many will give lip service to the notion of some sort of "personified evil force." Some will

---

1   David Nussman, "Most US Catholics Don't Believe in Devil," *Church Militant*, August 30, 2017, https://www.churchmilitant .com/news/article/most-us-catholics-dont-believe-in-devil.

admit with hesitation that the devil is at work in evil people. But the idea that the devil and demons actively work to damn the average person is beyond the pale.

The devil is a fallen angel, as is every demon. The account of the fall of Lucifer is in at least two places in the Old Testament:

> How art thou fallen from heaven, O Lucifer, who didst rise in the morning? how art thou fallen to the earth, that didst wound the nations? And thou saidst in thy heart: I will ascend into heaven, I will exalt my throne above the stars of God, I will sit in the mountain of the covenant, in the sides of the north. I will ascend above the height of the clouds, I will be like the most High. But yet thou shalt be brought down to hell, into the depth of the pit. They that shall see thee, shall turn toward thee, and behold thee. Is this the man that troubled the earth, that shook kingdoms, That made the world a wilderness, and destroyed the cities thereof, that opened not the prison to his prisoners? (Is. 14:12–17)

> Thou a cherub stretched out, and protecting, and I set thee in the holy mountain of God, thou hast walked in the midst of the stones of fire. Thou wast perfect in thy ways from the day of thy creation, until iniquity was found in thee. By the multitude of thy merchandise, thy inner parts were filled with iniquity, and thou hast sinned: and I cast thee out from the mountain of God, and destroyed thee, O covering cherub, out of the midst of the stones of fire. (Ez. 28:14–16)

In both of these passages from the Old Testament prophets, we see mention of the fallen angel Lucifer. Lucifer was highly regarded in the eyes of God, but due to pride, he was cast down as a punishment. Tradition and Scripture hold that Lucifer was the highest of angels, thus his fall was the most drastic. The expression "the corruption of the best is the worst" would apply to Lucifer. The name Lucifer means "morning star" or "bringer of light." It is ironic that other false religions speak of "enlightenment." It is also telling that the most philosophically absurd and morally degenerate era in the last one thousand years is called the Enlightenment. It makes you wonder from whence comes this source of "light."

The reality of the devil is a scriptural truth. Furthermore, one need only consult the experiences of exorcists and saints. To deny the reality of the devil is to deny the teachings of the Catholic Church, and to deny the teachings of the Church is to cease to be Catholic. For a Catholic, it isn't enough to simply acknowledge the existence of the devil any more than it isn't enough to simply acknowledge the existence of God. Understanding that God exists is the first step on the path to catholicity. But what we do with this belief is more important.

The devil believes in the existence of God but that was not enough to keep him in God's good graces. In fact, Satanists believe in God, and many of them even believe in the Real Presence of the Eucharist. This is why consecrated Hosts are often stolen for nefarious purposes. Sadly, the proliferation of Communion in the hand has made the stealing of Hosts more doable due to the careless nature in which many handle the Body of Christ. You need to live as though God is real and not be satisfied with mere belief. You prove the strength of your belief in God by going to Mass, frequenting the sacraments, and living a moral life. Since the active and destructive work of the devil is seen throughout the history of the faith, we ought to take it seriously and recognize that Satan's existence is a fact. Jesus

Christ dealt directly with the devil and went beyond simply acknowledging his existence, so we should act accordingly.

In the same manner, we must go beyond simple acknowledgment of the devil and make the transition from belief to action. The devil and his legions are constantly working to destroy your life, to tempt you to sin, and to bring you to hell. Therefore, you must be on the offense and not only be in a reactionary or defensive posture. Some people have told me that they think I am too extreme or paranoid when I speak about the devil as a relentless enemy. They are mistaken.

St. Peter tells us, "Be sober and watch: because your adversary the devil, as a roaring lion, goeth about seeking whom he may devour. Whom resist ye, strong in faith: knowing that the same affliction befalls your brethren who are in the world" (1 Pt. 5:8–9).

The first pope makes it clear that the devil is a predator, like a roaring lion. This means that he preys on the vulnerable and loves to make a show of his power. It also means that we resist the devil by staying strong, as predators do not go after those they cannot overcome. This passage also reminds us to not pay any attention to the roaring. The devil is like a mad man who seeks to intimidate by posturing with loud noises.

Furthermore, St. Peter tells us that the same affliction befalls your brethren who are in the world. The devil is after all of us, especially those of us who seek to live in God's good graces. All men are in the same situation in that they must resist the predator and pay no mind to his showmanship and pompous peacocking. We must support our brethren and remember that all of us may fall at any moment.

There is an episode of the show *The World's Deadliest Gangs* that follows a criminal who found his way into a prison gang. This man was a hardened criminal, and both inside and outside of jail, he made his living as a hit man for motorcycle gangs. At a certain point, he was put in jail for a considerable sentence and, like most hardened criminals, he sought refuge in the prison version of the gang to which he belonged on the outside. He estimates that in prison alone, he had killed more than twenty men. That being said, he was not completely without a moral code, as is no one (see Rom. 1:20–21).

At a certain point, this man heard of a hit set up outside of the prison to be carried out by a fellow gang member who was just released. This criminal associate was tasked with murdering the wife and child of a rival gang member. Even in this world of unspeakable sin, the man profiled in this television show felt the prick of his conscience and made it clear to the gang hierarchy that he would no longer be a part of the organization. He was going rogue. He was fine with the collateral damage of gang warfare, but he would not involve innocent women and children. And they say there is no honor among thieves! In any case, as you can imagine, this made him a marked man. He found himself stuck inside the walls of a prison full of some of the most dangerous people on earth, many of whom wanted him dead. He couldn't join another gang, because prison gangs usually separate along racial lines. He couldn't start his own gang, because the sheer power of opposition was too strong. His only option was to fend for himself. At a certain point in the show, the interviewer asked the man while they were walking around the prison yard, "Some would say you are being paranoid, what do you say to that?" His reply, "I am not paranoid. I am hyper vigilant. I know everyone here wants to kill me, so I act accordingly."

It may seem odd to include this example from a show about gangsters and murderers. But there are more similarities between you and this man than you think. None of us are without sin, and at one point, even if in infancy, we were all part of the devil's gang. At baptism, we were pulled out of the devil's ranks and he has been after us ever since. Some of us have done horrible things, while some of us have remained closer to the straight and narrow path. No matter; in the eyes of the devil, all of us have defected from his camp and have gone rogue. Like the man from this show, we are not being paranoid if we think the devil is under every rock. We might be mistaken at times, but we aren't being paranoid. We are showing hyper vigilance by acknowledging that there are demonic criminals all around us who seek the ruin of our soul, like the St. Michael prayer so clearly says.

Now, luckily for us, we are not required to do this on our own. In fact, if we return to the passage from St. Peter, we see the first pope went on to say, "But the God of all grace, who hath called us unto his eternal glory in Christ Jesus, after you have suffered a little, will himself perfect you, and confirm you, and establish you" (1 Pt. 5:10). St. Peter does an incredible job demonstrating to us how we are to deal with the devil.

Firstly, he makes it very clear that we are to stay sober. This means that we must keep a clear mind and stay free from sins that take away our ability to reason. Secondly, he reminds us of the predatory nature of the devil. Thus, we should stand on guard, as the devil spends his time searching out our ruin. Thirdly, he tells us that our brothers experience the same travail and that we must remain strong. Finally, he explains to us that it is from God that we receive the grace necessary to withstand the evil one. Our temporal suffering by way of temptation and spiritual battle is ordained for our perfection. Through triumph over trials, we may establish ourselves amongst the elect who spend eternity with God.

It is simply a fact that the devil is constantly after you, and the sooner you recognize this fact, the sooner you can get to work.

How Do We Defend Ourselves?

"Have courage and do not fear the assaults of the devil. Remember this forever; it is a healthy sign if the devil shouts and roars around your conscience, since this shows that he is not inside your will."

—St. Padre Pio

The simplest way to defend ourselves from Satan is to stay in a *state of grace.* This entire book is geared toward helping you live in a state of grace and thrive as part of the Church Militant. To be in a state of grace, we need to avoid committing *mortal sins*, and if we do commit them, we need to go to confession as soon as possible. When we commit a mortal sin, we essentially open a door to the demonic. This greatly weakens us in our efforts to defend against temptation, and over time, our intellect is darkened. Is it any wonder why our society seems insane? Given the proliferation of grave sins such as pornography and fornication—which many participate in often—it is likely that a large portion of people are persisting in sinful lifestyles that they know are wrong. Whether or not someone has full knowledge of each individual sin, we can't know, but we know that Saint Paul attests to the inborn nature of the moral law in the hearts of all men when he compares Jews and Gentiles: "Who shew the work of the law written in their hearts, *their conscience bearing witness to them*, and their thoughts between themselves accusing, or also defending one another" (Rom 2:15, emphasis added). Whole swaths of people are literally less intelligent than they would otherwise be. Our society is sinful, therefore our society is stupid.

Mortal sins are serious sins that reject the indwelling of the Holy Trinity in our soul. The word *mortal* has its root in the word *mors*, which is the Latin word for death. When we commit a mortal sin, we are no longer in friendship with God and there is no room for God to dwell in our hearts. Mortal sin destroys in our soul the virtue of charity that is infused at Baptism and renewed by the sacrament of confession. The virtue of charity is our union with God. The Council of Trent declared that we maintain the virtues of faith and hope after we commit a mortal sin, both of which encourage us to seek out the sacrament of confession. But the *Catechism of the Council of Trent* explains that "whoever offends God, even by one mortal sin, instantly forfeits whatever merits he may have previously acquired through the sufferings and death of Christ, and is entirely shut out from the gates of heaven." Just one unconfessed mortal sin is sufficient for damnation and eternal hellfire. This is because we have broken our relationship with God through charity. Thus, we should clarify the three stipulations required in order to meet the criteria for a sin to be mortal:

1. *Serious or grave matter.* This often means that the action is clearly evil or severely disordered. This would include many common activities: looking at evil images, contraception, intentionally missing Mass, recreational drug use, etc.

2. *Sufficient knowledge or reflection.* This means we know we are committing a sinful act and that we have had sufficient reflection for it to be intentional. Some may tell you that the knowledge portion renders most sins less serious than a mortal sin because most people do not have a knowledge of the Faith. It is worth nothing that knowledge does *not* mean understanding. Furthermore, nowhere in any dogmatic teaching or Scripture does it say that we must have specific theological knowledge in order to commit mortal sin. Everyone is born with a sense of the natural law, meaning that an understanding of morality, even if imperfect, is built into our nature. St. Paul says, "All have sinned, and do need the glory of God, being justified freely by his grace, through the redemption, that is in Christ Jesus" (Rom. 3:23–24).

3. *Full consent of the will.* This means that we must freely choose to commit a grave sin in order for it to be a mortal sin. If there is any significant impediment to our will, then it is possible that the sin is not mortal but only venial (venial sins are less serious sins).

How to Distinguish Mortal and Venial Sins

"To be silent when we are impelled to utter words injurious to God or to our neighbour, is an act of virtue; but to be silent in confessing our sins is the ruin of the soul."

—St. Alphonsus

It is true that at times we may not be certain if we have met the three necessary criteria. In this case, I would err on the side of caution and confess the sin. In fact, even venial sins should be confessed in order to gain graces to stop committing any sin at all. For example, I work with many other people, which means I need to be on guard against gossip and harmful backbiting. There have been times where I have at least passively participated in conversations that were rife with gossip. If I actively participated with the intent of denigrating someone's character, then I could have committed the mortal sin of detraction—seeking to destroy a reputation. On the other hand, if I passively tolerated the insults and gossip, then I would be committing a venial sin rather than a mortal sin. This is because I didn't fully participate in the sinful activity, but I failed to act virtuously. In this case, I would bring this to confession in order to obtain the graces to stop participating in gossip altogether. This is a little known fact about the sacrament: confession not only cleanses mortal sin but also gives grace to overcome sin in the future.

It is possible for a sin to be mortal in one circumstance and venial in another. It should be noted, however, that, as already stated from the *Catechism of the Council of Trent*, only one mortal sin is necessary for us to forfeit heaven.

Most of our sins are not mortal, but virtually all people commit at least one mortal sin, if not more, throughout their life. Do not hedge your bets, and move swiftly to the sacrament of confession if you have any doubts. God will be pleased with your fervor for holiness, and you will grow closer to him through your efforts. Only be careful to guard yourself against the vice of scrupulosity.

Everyone has sinned (excluding Our Lord and Our Lady), and everyone is in need of redemption. The crucifixion of Our Lord Jesus Christ was for you as much as for anyone who has ever lived. There are some saints who have lived lives free of mortal sin, like St. Thérèse de Lisieux, but this is the exception. Do not count yourself among the exceptions. Ironically, the greatest saints who lived free of mortal sin viewed themselves as wretched sinners. Their humility propelled them to always rely on God's mercy in the confessional. St. Dominic Savio, a young pupil of St. John Bosco, died as a young boy who seems to have never committed a mortal sin. He had a motto: *Death before sin!* Adopt this motto, make it your own, and repeat it to yourself when tempted by the devil.

In later chapters, we will discuss specific ways to arm ourselves and our homes against the demonic, as well as ways to fortify ourselves against temptations to sin.

Ignorance Is Not Bliss

"Yes, dear Lord, if all the tortures that captives undergo in this land, if all the stark intensity of their sufferings should be my lot, I offer myself for it with all my heart."

—St. Jean de Brebeuf

There is no salvation outside of the Catholic Church. This is a hard teaching but a teaching nonetheless. In ages past, this was understood with clarity and conviction. Sadly, many Catholic laymen and clerics are made squeamish by this doctrine. However, it is the foundational truth that drives all missionary zeal and the desire to convert sinners. If the Catholic Church is not the only ark of salvation, then we can dispense with the demands of the one true Faith. Jesus Christ makes this very clear when he says, "I am the way, and the truth, and the life. No man cometh to the Father, but by me" (Jn. 14:6). Notice he does not say, "I am one of the truths, I am one of the ways." Jesus Christ is the only Savior, the only Messiah.

Without Christ, we are all damned, and we must accept this hard truth in order to see God face to face. Furthermore, Christ established the Catholic Church. Our Church is not an invisible assembly of anonymous Christians; it is a visible Church with sacraments and a hierarchy. There are things we must believe in order to be Catholic. Mere belief in Jesus Christ as Lord is not enough, regardless of what many Christians may profess. Catholic missionaries of the past understood this.

The North American Martyrs, including St. Jean de Brebeuf, St. Isaac Jogues, and their companions, all died brutal deaths for the conversion of the native inhabitants they encountered. These men traveled across the Atlantic ocean and walked thousands of kilometers throughout the Great Lakes region. They did so in order that they might convert the pagan aboriginals, specifically the Huron, Algonquin, and Iroquois tribes.

At first, they had relative success in converting the Algonquins, but the Huron and Iroquois tribes were more hostile. Our insane culture has labeled all missionaries of the past as colonizers who sought to forcefully impose a civilization on the native people. But this is historically inaccurate when you analyze the lives of the martyrs. They wintered with the Algonquin tribe and adapted to their way of life. They lived in their dwellings, ate their food, and learned their crafts. Meanwhile, they taught them the Catholic faith, bringing them to baptism and saving their souls. If the North American Martyrs were concerned with any sort of colonization, it was a colonization of salvation.

Initially, Brebeuf had very little success with the Huron tribe, and because of this, he returned home, only to return years later. Throughout his unsuccessful first journey, he lived in extreme hardship, often going days without food. Why on earth did he return to such a tumultuous existence? He did so because he believed, rightly so, that the native people were at great risk of damnation if they were not baptized and incorporated into the Roman Catholic Church.

Speaking of their evangelization method, Brebeuf wrote that they began their catechizing efforts with the memorable truth that at death the immortal soul is separated from the body, going either to heaven or to hell. If you are ever told that it is uncharitable to speak so plainly of damnation in evangelization efforts, please disregard that nonsense. True Christian charity desires the salvation of every soul. How can we preach the Good News if we do not make clear the bad news?

On one occasion, St. Isaac Jogues and a companion were captured by the Iroquois and beaten severely with knotted sticks. Their hair, beards, and nails were torn off, and their forefingers were bitten through. The Iroquois bit off the priests's index fingers and thumbs to render them incapable of offering the Holy Sacrifice of the Mass. However, Pope Urban VIII granted Jogues special permission to offer Mass with mutilated hands, saying, "It would be unjust that a martyr for Christ should not drink the Blood of Christ." Some years into his journey, St. Isaac Jogues suffered martyrdom at the hands of the Iroquois when they hacked off his head with a tomahawk. After the death of Jogues, the Iroquois attacked the Huron community where St. Jean de Brebeuf was living. Brebeuf had experienced much more success on his second attempt with the Hurons than on his previous. They were converting and coming to know Our Lord through the sacraments.

The torture of St. Jean de Brebeuf and his companion at the hands of the Iroquois was as heinous as anything you could imagine. Through the humiliation of having every inch of their naked bodies beaten with sticks, St. Jean de Brebeuf continued to comfort his newly found spiritual children who witnessed his passion. Hatchets heated to a red-hot temperature were applied under their armpits and beside their bowels. Necklaces of smoldering blades were placed around their necks. The sadistic torturers then girdled them with bark soaked in pitch and resin (fire igniting liquids) and set them ablaze. Through all of this, St. Jean de Brebeuf continued to preach the Gospel and to offer his life as a passion for the souls of the natives. The Iroquois were so enraged by the saving truth of Jesus Christ that they cut off his nose, gagged his mouth, and tore off his lips. The persecutors went on to inundate him and his priest companion with boiling water as a type of diabolical baptism. Large pieces of the priests' flesh were cut off their living bodies and roasted as food, again to mock the Blessed Sacrament of the Most Holy Eucharist. The martyrs finally died as their hearts were cut out of their chests while they were still living. Like St. Longinus, the Roman centurion who thrust the spear into the side of Christ, the persecutors and tribes who witnessed this death converted to the one true Faith.

We spit in the face of the North American Martyrs if we pretend that salvation is achieved by all. We make a mockery of their martyrdom if we spread the foolish notion that ignorance of Christ excuses a man from hellfire. St. Jean, St. Isaac, and their companions gave of themselves in the most gruesome of fashions in order to save just one soul. They knew that ignorance is not bliss and that only one unconfessed mortal sin or unbaptized soul can make a man the eternal property of the prince of darkness. Do not fall for the devil's deception that all religions are sufficient for salvation. Waste not even a moment with the absurd notion that ignorance excuses a man from his sins.

2

EFFEMINATE MEN

"Know you not that the unjust shall not possess the kingdom of God? Do not err: neither fornicators, nor idolaters, nor adulterers, nor the effeminate, nor liars with mankind, nor thieves, nor covetous, nor drunkards, nor railers, nor extortioners, shall possess the kingdom of God."

—1 Corinthians 6:9–10

"And he took away the effeminate out of the land, and he removed all the filth of the idols, which his fathers had made."

—3 Kings 15:12

EFFEMINACY does not mean "femininity," as femininity is a perfection, like masculinity. Effeminacy is a different word entirely, and in its etymology, we find a definition for things like "softness" in its Latin usage. The Greek word for effeminacy in the New Testament is *malakia* (μαλακία), which means "softness."

St. Thomas defines effeminacy as a reluctance to suffer due to an attachment to pleasure. He explains that effeminacy is a vice opposed to perseverance. In essence, effeminacy is a vice that is opposed to the cross, which is an unfortunate characteristic that might explain the multitude of soft men who reject life's redemptive sufferings in pursuit of temporal pleasure.

21

Our society is full of effeminate men. This is evident in the rampant softness of the average man and the fakery of so-called men that flood our celebrity culture and political landscapes. One needn't look much further than Canadian prime minister Justin Trudeau, a man who does his best to pose with drag queens at every opportunity. The fact that a man like him is the face of my country shows just how far our society has declined in virtue. Canada is a nation traditionally known for lumberjacks, strong beer, rugged winters, and hockey fights. Instead of a great leader, my beloved nation has suffered through a man who seems more interested in auditioning for a boy band than leading a country.

Effeminacy is a plague, and it must be eradicated. Today's men are on average softer than a soiled diaper, and like a soiled diaper, our society does its best to render men disposable. Traditional personality traits of boyhood have been labeled symptoms of ADHD. The natural and manly inclination to take personal responsibility and *fight* for what is truly just has been usurped by social justice activism. Men used to be adept at hunting and animal husbandry, but now many men would rather spend their time protesting KFC and eating a soy burger.

What Are the Roots of Effeminacy?

"The real man is the man of virtue. With virtue comes interior self-discipline and self-control. It is the hallmark of a real man. He can engage in things that are hard and arduous and still remain steadfast. A man who wilts is effeminate."

—Exorcist Fr. Chad Ripperger

As with all sinfulness, we find ourselves looking to the Fall, when sin entered the world through the actions of Adam and Eve. St. Thomas, along with other saints and theologians, states that the original sin is pride. This should give us pause when we see pride as something worthy of a parade. Could there be anything more offensive to God than to celebrate the most fundamental of sins with a display that glorifies sexual deviancy?

At any rate, the original sin is pride, which is the primary sin of Adam and Eve. Pride is traditionally defined as a desire to *exalt oneself beyond what is appropriate for one's state or condition.* This is demonstrated in the third chapter of Genesis as the Serpent tempts Eve. The devil says, "For God doth know that in what day soever you shall eat thereof, your eyes shall be opened: and you shall be as gods, knowing good and evil" (Gen. 3:5). Eve is attracted to the possibility of seeking equality with God, which is the sin that cast Lucifer out of heaven in the first place.

There are capital sins or vices, like pride or envy, and there exists what are called the daughters, or sub-sins. Lust is a capital sin, and self-love is a daughter, or sub-sin, of lust. We can look to the characteristics of the sub-sins in order to identify the root capital sin. For example, lust is an inappropriate sexual desire, but it is also a strong disordered passion for something for the sake of pleasure. That's why we can say things like "blood lust." If you were to do a self-examination of your virtues and vices and you found that you struggled with impulsiveness or self-love, then it is likely that you have difficulties with controlling lustful appetites. This is because both of these sub-sins tend to fall under lust.

Also, it is possible to commit more than one capital sin at a time, like when someone commits adultery. Adultery includes the sin of lust but also the sin of covetousness, as it is the act of coveting something that belongs to another. Understanding the categorization of sin is helpful for our own spiritual lives. By properly categorizing the nature of certain sins, we can properly analyze the root effeminacy in the original sin.

Effeminacy Destroys Male-Female Order

"There is, nonetheless, an inbuilt nature in women to subordi-nate themselves to rightly-ordered authority—if the husband holds this authority the wife will have a desire to please him."

—Exorcist Fr. Chad Ripperger

Adam and Eve were created at the beginning of time with a properly ordered marital relationship. It is an unpopular teaching, even amongst many conservative Catholics today, but men are ordained to be the head of the marital relationship: "But I would have you know, that the head of every man is Christ; and the head of the woman is the man; and the head of Christ is God" (1 Cor. 11:3). This headship is based on obedience to Christ, who demonstrates obedience to God the Father. It is not an arbitrary headship but instead an acknowledgment of dominion, which we find in the first chapter of Genesis.

The word *dominion* refers to a special sort of authority over the totality of things. This is why we use the word *dominate*, which stems from the same root word, when we speak of someone totally controlling an opponent for example. Of course, this is not to suggest that men are to dominate women or anything of the sort. In fact, this dominion over creation was given to both men and women. This is one reason why we need to be skeptical of vegetarian or animal rights movements as Catholics. Any implied equality between man and the beasts is against divine revelation. In any case, dominion is given to Adam and Eve, and man is called to headship. Adam and Eve share dominion, yet Adam holds a dominion that Eve does not share. Furthermore, St. Paul clearly explains what the family dynamic is supposed to look like in Ephesians:

> Being subject one to another, in the fear of Christ. Let women be subject to their husbands, as to the Lord: Because the husband is the head of the wife, as Christ is the head of the church. He is the saviour of his body. Therefore as the church is subject to Christ, so also let the wives be to their husbands in all things.
>
> Husbands, love your wives, as Christ also loved the church, and delivered himself up for it: That he might sanctify it, cleansing it by the laver of water in the word of life: That he might present it to himself a glorious church, not having spot or wrinkle, or any such thing; but that it should be holy, and without blemish. So also ought men to love their wives as their own bodies. He that loveth his wife, loveth himself. For no man ever hated his own flesh; but nourisheth and cherisheth it, as also Christ doth the church. Because we are members of his body, of his flesh, and of his bones.

> For this cause shall a man leave his father and mother: and shall cleave to his wife. And they shall be two in one flesh. This is a great sacrament: but I speak in Christ and in the church. Nevertheless, let every one of you in particular love his wife as himself: and let the wife fear her husband. (Eph. 5:21–33)

There are three main points in this teaching from St. Paul that illustrate the proper roles of man and woman in marriage. Understanding this will help us to better understand Adam's sin of effeminacy as well as Eve's sin of disobedience or usurpation, what we today call feminism.

1. Man and wife are called to submit to one another out of reverence for Christ. This means that our bodies cease to be our own at the consummation of marriage; therefore, we belong to our spouse. Our wedding vows oblige us to an openness to life and to marital fidelity. We sanctify each other through the sacrament of Matrimony. In order to participate with the graces of the sacrament, we must live out the teachings faithfully. Contraception usage, even in marriage, is a grave sin and must be confessed. This should caution men about "not wanting any more kids," which is an uncatholic proposition. Our bodies are not our own and we owe our wives everything, even unlimited fatherhood.

2. After the spiritual or sacramental submission of both man and woman is established, we have a foundational "governmental" structure in the home. We are not just spiritual creatures but also physical. This means we need to interact with and operate in

the material world. Families need to be taken care of, children need to be raised, and homes need to be cared for. One of the most unfortunate consequences of the so-called equality we have today is that our roles are completely distorted. This disorder greatly affects family life. There is a remarkable difference in the spiritual and physical ambience of a home where the wife is home with the children as compared to the opposite. There is even a tangible difference in the spiritual protection of a traditional home versus the average two-income home. Demons hate rightly ordered marriage, which is why the devil first attacked the marital bond between Adam and Eve. A rightly ordered home is a sign that the devil is not welcome. At any rate, due to many biological and spiritual factors, men and women have been ordained with different roles in marriage for very practical reasons. This requires headship by the husband.

3. Men are called to lead as Christ led. It should be obvious what this means: men are called to die in self-sacrificial service to their bride as Christ did for the Church. This is yet another thing that our society completely misunderstands. Men are designed for leadership, and this cannot be established unless they are allowed to lead. Anyone who has ever coached a team will tell you that it is necessary to have one captain, one head coach, and one voice in times of crisis. In fact, submission to leadership actually facilitates creativity and freedom as proper order is established. Women are

free to be women, and men are free to be men in a marriage where men act like Christ. By dying to themselves in service to their wives and children, men allow their families to live in true freedom. Problems arise when women do not submit to their husbands and when men do not lead their wives. It would be like the Church not submitting to Christ and Christ abandoning his cross.

This explains why the Fall was a prime example of marital confusion, with a usurpation of leadership by Eve and a neglect of duty and service by Adam. Satan sought to converse with Eve rather than Adam because he sought to destroy marriage by flipping the marital order. Adam is charged with leadership and Eve is his *helper* (see Gen. 2:20). This means that Eve is supposed to help Adam in his responsibilities as the head of the home. Men and women are to perform tasks proper to their state, which acts as a guard against delegating responsibilities without necessity. There is a hierarchy of duties and responsibilities in marriage; many are interchangeable, like household chores, but some are distinctly ordained to husband or wife.

Many modern men and women like to feign a brand of equality or feminism when they speak of the roles in marriage. But no one in their right mind would suggest that the wife should confront an intruder in the home while the man stands and does nothing. This is exactly the scene we see in the Garden of Eden. Satan is a snake who needs to be booted out of the Garden. Adam should be driving him out and calling on St. Michael to behead the unjust usurper. Furthermore, Eve should seek her husband's counsel in the matter and should not deal with this situation on her own. All outside influences on a home are a potential threat to the family. For this reason, husbands need to take ownership of all decisions that are made between the world and the home. Only once a threat has been avoided or neutralized should a husband delegate responsibility to his wife. This is to ensure the safety and prosperity of the home.

Effeminate Men Flee Danger

"And fear ye not them that kill the body, and are not able to kill the soul: but rather fear him that can destroy both soul and body in hell."

—Matthew 10:28

Even though the traditional biblical languages are in certain cases difficult to translate properly into English, they are the closest to the original text. Hence a traditional Catholic translation of the Holy Bible, like the Douay-Rheims or Knox Holy Bible, is highly recommended. The dialogue with the devil is best translated in the Douay-Rheims, where the devil says to Eve, "No, you shall not die the death" (Gen. 3:4). When the devil says *you shall not die the death*, he seeks to foment confusion about the death of body and soul.

The devil tempts Eve to a rationalization of mortal sin (death of the soul), something common to many. Adam and Eve were created immortal, but it is not the case that they were created invincible, as they had human bodies. Nevertheless, bodily death by decay is the result of sin and did not exist before the Fall. They were created in a state of perfection and contained a type of perfect human knowledge and mystical union with God. They had full knowledge of the reality of sin and virtue. Notice that Eve says to the Serpent, "We should not touch it, lest perhaps we die" (Gen. 3:3). Immediately, the devil seeks to twist the meaning of death and the commandments of God in his dialogue with Eve. Eve is greatly tempted by the fruit because it is "fair to the eyes, and delightful to behold" (Gen. 3:6). She is pulled by great sensory pleasure in her contemplation of the fruit and seeks satisfaction of a bodily pleasure in her consumption of that which is forbidden. We see here the sin that the Blessed Mother completely reverses when she demonstrates perfect chastity and detachment from carnal things. Eve listens to the serpent and rationalizes her desire for bodily pleasure, thereby justifying disobedience to God.

Throughout this dialogue with the devil, Adam is standing beside Eve. This is clear because of the fact that Eve immediately "gave to her husband who did eat" (Gen. 3:6). Eve has already sinned, but Adam is the spiritual head of the human race through his primordial fatherhood. We are told by Saint Augustine that "the deliberate sin of the first man is the cause of original sin."[1] Saint Anselm adds: "the sin of Adam was one thing but the sin of children at their birth is quite another, the former was the cause, the latter is the effect."[2] What this means is if he were to avoid partaking in the forbidden fruit, then his children would not have contracted the spiritual disease now implicit in his patrimony. This should illuminate for us the great

---

1   *De Nuptiis Et Concupiscentia*, II, xxvi, 43.
2   *De Conceptu Virginali*, xxvi.

power we have as men in our homes. We could say that we facilitate the transmission of sin, but we also sanctify our families through spiritual leadership. Adam is ultimately guilty of the original sin due to his negation of responsibility and willful neglect of what is proper to his nature as a man. Instead of standing by, he should have demonstrated self-sacrifice and death to self.

Of course, women are required to die to self and to sacrifice, but these virtues are to be demonstrated differently. It is not proper to Eve as a woman to deal with an intruder, as she does not have ultimate authority over the home. Furthermore, man and woman are created with a complementary nature. We are predisposed to different perfections that facilitate a certain perfection in marriage and family. It is proper to her nature that Eve should be vulnerable to this sort of temptation. Women are designed to seek what is pleasing and to share with their husbands. Furthermore, women are made to be relational and to more easily see the good in a given situation. This inherent optimism is a useful characteristic when rearing children. In essence, Eve is doing what one would expect. In her dialogue with the devil, she seeks a verbal remedy to the situation rather than a confrontational or physical one.

At the Fall, our first parents are in a state of spiritual perfection; therefore, they have perfect regulation of their emotions and passions. This means that Adam has full reflection and consent to his passivity, meaning he could have acted with impunity in a righteously violent manner.

The Rosary Defends Against Effeminacy

*"And when he had made, as it were, a scourge of little cords,
he drove them all out of the temple, the sheep also and the oxen,
and the money of the changers he poured out, and the tables he
overthrew."*

—St. John 2:15

The Gospel according to St. John puts forth in the first
two chapters a replaying or representation of the creation
by way of the coming of Christ. In Genesis 1:4–5, we see
God's recognition of the goodness of light and the separation of the light from the darkness. This refers to not only
a physical reality but also an event. This is the separation
between the fallen demons and the good angels after Lucifer rejects the call to submit to God. John 1:4–5 refers to the
life that is in Christ that is the "light of men," and that "the
light shineth in darkness, and the darkness did not compre-
hend it."

John's Gospel is a theological masterpiece, as he shows
the fulfillment of all things in Christ, starting with the creation. In chapter two of John, we see the wedding at Cana,
which alludes to the marriage of Adam and Eve in the second chapter of Genesis. At this wedding, we see six jars
of water that become wine, which refer to the six days of
creation. We also see Mary, the New Eve, as the first to
speak when approached by the servants at the feast, and out
of obedience, she defers directly to Jesus, the New Adam.
After the wedding has concluded, John brings us to a scene
in the Temple where Jesus famously cleanses it of vendors
and money changers. The Temple prefigures the Church,
but it could also be said that the marriage prefigures the

Temple and is fulfilled by the Church and her Mass. This is one reason why Christ refers to himself as the Bridegroom. The marriage of Adam and Eve constituted the first domestic Church. In this Church, or his "Father's house," Adam allows the devil to sell his corrupt goods to his wife.

Like in Genesis, where Adam observes the situation before taking action, Christ does this as well. In John 2:14 Jesus "found in the temple them that sold oxen and sheep and doves, and the changers of money sitting." In Genesis, we can imagine Adam happening upon his wife and observing the infernal money changer offering his sinful commodities. John 2:15 says that Jesus "made, as it were, a scourge of little cords, he drove them all out of the temple." This means that Jesus took the time to weave a handmade whip to inflict serious pain. I do not know how long this would have taken, but nonetheless, it was an intentional manufacturing of a weapon that he fully intended to use with force and purpose.

This scourge can be seen as a prefiguration of the Most Holy Rosary of the Blessed Virgin Mary. John describes it as a "scourge of little cords," which means a small hand-held weapon that is either knotted or put together with small fragments akin to beads. Christ shows us in this instance that when we wield the Rosary as our weapon to clear out our homes, we wield the power of Christ through the intercession of Mary.

This is the appropriate response to an intruder in your domestic church! Adam did the opposite and partook in the corrupt economy of sin.

When we seek to appease our wife and partake in the sin that she offers us, as Adam did, we commit the greater sin. Woman was created to be presented to man as a gift, and man was created to guard and protect her as a precious helpmate and dependent. Eve is duped by the devil, but her vulnerability is magnified by Adam's effeminate example. Instead of forging a scourge to whip the devil, Adam appeases his wife by avoiding confrontation with the serpent. The maxim "happy wife, happy life" could not be further from the truth. Instead, we should be saying "holy wife, happy life." Worldly happiness is fleeting. It profits a man nothing to gain temporal peace in his home by appeasement of his wife if it means eternal damnation of his family by shaking hands with the devil.

The Blame Game

"If, then, we are not to blame for the thing that we are accused of, we are never wholly without blame in the way that our good Jesus was."

—St. Teresa of Avila

Adam shows us the roots of effeminacy and Eve shows the roots of feminism in their solitary act of disobedience to God. Our culture is rife with disordered marriage as men constantly groan "yes dear" while they rot away drooling in front of the television. When God confronts Adam after the sin, he says, "Where art thou" (Gen. 3:9), a question that has nothing to do with geography. The appropriate response from Adam would have been, "I have cut myself off from you, Lord, and find myself lost." However, Adam explicitly states he is afraid and therefore hid himself (see Gen. 3:10).

Now, the fear of God *is* the beginning of wisdom as the proverb tells us (see Prov. 1:7); therefore, fear of God and fear of losing God after mortal sin is an appropriate response. But Adam shows us the disordered conduct that plagues men when they submit to their wives in an improper leadership of the home. When God inquires as to the eating of the forbidden fruit, Adam replies, "The woman, whom thou gavest me to be my companion, gave me of the tree, and I did eat" (Gen. 3:12).

Blaming someone else, especially your spouse, is a sure sign of effeminate behavior. How many times have we seen this? A man develops an addiction to evil images, and when confronted by his wife, he expresses that she hasn't "met his needs." Or a man realizes that the finances in his home are in disarray. Rather than take responsibility for his poor financial stewardship, he blames her shopping or the renovation she "made him do."

Look, you are Adam; your home is your garden. Everything is your responsibility, and all failures will be worked out on your shoulders. The goal for men is to go from being the old Adam to the new Adam. As a punishment, but also a penance, the Lord said to Adam: "Because thou hast hearkened to the voice of thy wife . . . cursed is the earth in thy work; with labour and toil shalt thou eat thereof all the days of thy life" (Gen. 3:17). Furthermore, Adam's work will be among "thorns and thistles" (v. 18) and "in the sweat of thy face shalt thou eat bread" (v. 19). This is a prefigurement of the new Adam, Jesus Christ, and his work to reverse the original sin. Christ does this with an act of humility so great that he allows himself to be mocked with a crown of thorns. Also, the Passion begins with the Agony in the

Garden and the sweating of blood from the great weight of sin. Among thorns, our Lord works out our salvation by the bloody sweat of his brow.

If we are to transition from the old Adam to the new, we must work tirelessly all the days of our life. We must work among the thorns of sin, and our sacrifice should be so great that we are prepared to shed our own blood to provide for our families. This does not only include financial and material provision. Most importantly, we must renew our commitment daily to take up our rosary and use it as a scourge to beat the infernal merchant of sin out of our temple. We must stand in front of Eve and attach ourselves to the tree of life as we accept the nails of iniquity through our limbs. As Christ hung on the tree of death at Calvary, he opened his side by allowing St. Longinus to stick him through with a spear. We must seek to do the same.

The Crucifixion is not merely an event in history but a model we must use to crush the emissary of effeminacy who seeks to drag us into the pit.

3

TAME THE HORSE

"And every one that striveth for the mastery, refraineth himself from all things: and they indeed that they may receive a corruptible crown; but we an incorruptible one. I therefore so run, not as at uncertainty: I so fight, not as one beating the air: But I chastise my body, and bring it into subjection: lest perhaps, when I have preached to others, I myself should become a castaway."

—1 Corinthians 9:25–27

"But a beast that may be sacrificed to the Lord, if any one shall vow, shall be holy."

—Leviticus 27:9

THERE is an animated movie called *Spirit: Stallion of the Cimarron* that I have watched with my eldest sons. It is a wholesome film, and it teaches my boys a decent lesson about what it takes to *tame the horse*. In a nutshell, the film is about a wild horse and a Native American man who go through an adventure together. They navigate their way through the wild and open wilderness of the burgeoning American civilization.

Both the man and the horse are prideful to begin with but also extremely driven and strong. Neither the horse nor the man are willing to be tamed by anyone. Their unfettered energy and compulsion lead them into trouble time and time again. By the end of the film, the two characters have gone through a series of death-defying exploits, and both have tamed each other. They realize that by taming their passions and ordering them toward a common goal, they can work together and flourish. Neither the horse nor the man threw away anything vital about themselves but instead trimmed away excessive pride that was unhelpful.

Man is made of body and soul, which means we are physical and metaphysical beings—body and spirit. Our bodies are material and interact with the natural world, and our souls are immaterial and interact with the supernatural world. Our souls also interact with the physical world in union with our bodies. This is why St. Paul says, "But he that committeth fornication, sinneth against his own body" (1 Cor. 6:18).

At the beginning of Genesis, it states, "In the beginning God created heaven and earth." This refers to not only a cosmological creation but also the creation of the angelic and the corporeal—that is, the spiritual and bodily creatures. We are a unique creature in the eyes of God, as we are made in his image. God the Father is pure spirit, but the imagistic similarity is in our soul, which contains our intellect and will. Our free will and ability to reason separate us from the animals who have bodies without rational souls.

Catholics are not dualists. We do not believe that there is a spiritual reality and a physical reality that are separated or in competition with one another. Of course, there is a spiritual realm and a physical realm; however, our faith is *incarnational*. God became man, hence the natural world is ordained to be good and not arbitrarily tossed away. This helps to explain why the supreme act of worship, Holy Mass, ignites all our physical and spiritual senses. Not only our souls but also our bodies are called to a pursuit of perfection.

Our human nature is fallen; therefore, our bodies are corrupt. We do not idolize our bodies and hold an arbitrary level of performance or health as a standard of holiness. Instead, we must subjugate the passions of our flesh to the rightly ordered reason of our will and our intellect. In essence, there is something like a master and servant relationship between the soul and the body. If the master is good, the servant will obey willingly and flourish. If the servant is good, the master will thrive and grow in virtue.

I have ridden a horse only once in my life, as a small child, so I am no authority on equestrian matters. However, in speaking to people who have mastered horse riding, they tell me that mastery of the horse creates a unique bond. It is as if they are one substance working together in harmony. In a way, the horse and the rider become like one person, each with their will and personalities working toward the same goal. If the rider does not tame the horse, then riding the horse is a disaster. Conversely, if the horse does not obey, he will never learn the magnificent things that experienced horse riders can make a horse do.

Those who train horses will tell you that there is an aspect of tender treatment that is necessary for the horse. But just as important is the *breaking* of the horse. Horses, like ourselves, come with different temperaments and therefore react differently to the breaking-in process. In the aforementioned movie, the horse is especially stubborn and requires repeated effort and even extreme measures to be broken-in. However, once his wild and physically dominant nature is tamed, he becomes the greatest companion and partner of the man who rides him.

We all have different temperaments, but I imagine that, at least to a degree, we all struggle with similar things. Some of us tend to be a little more virile or have a certain "fire in the belly." This can be great in contact sports or business but makes controlling lust and anger difficult. Some of us may have a handle on lust and anger but fall prey to video game addiction or drinking. Others may not have many issues with physical sinfulness yet struggle with slothfulness and indifference. Further still, some of us may have a certain neurosis and fail to see the joys in any sort of rightly ordered bodily pleasure. Whatever type of "horse" our body gives us, our soul must tame the horse so that we can ride in union with both parts of our nature. This is a sure way to accomplish the goals God has ordained for us.

In a fallen world, there is no fairness in biology, so it is useless to complain or bemoan things as they have come to us. If you struggle with obesity, then you have been given a cross to bear that can lead to heroic virtue. If you struggle with substance abuse, then you also have been given a burden that needs lifting. I have always struggled with an excessive love of violence, and if not for a high-contact sporting routine as a young man, I am sure I could have encountered legal trouble. I cannot allow myself to go any significant length of time without intense physical effort, otherwise I become like a dog who has not been walked— an ornery and volatile dog at that.

The Holy Bible tells us, "A horse not broken becometh stubborn, and a child left to himself will become headstrong" (Ecclus. 30:8). We all fall short compared to the glory of God, so instead of complaining about our lot in life, it is time that we put in the effort.

Time to Get Up!

"Arise, my glory; arise, psaltery and harp: I will arise in the morning early."

—Psalm 107:3

At 4:20 every morning, my alarm goes off with a preset alarm sound called "Early Riser." Thankfully, it is a low and peaceful sound that progresses from soft to loud over a series of minutes. This is vital, as I hear it before my wife does and therefore refrain from waking her. Most nights, I am asleep by 11:00, but with small children, someone is always teething, breastfeeding, wetting the bed, having nightmares, fighting a cold, or simply crying for no apparent reason. There are some nights throughout which I sleep the full five or more hours, but this is the exception. Out of twenty-four hours, I therefore sleep between roughly four and five hours on the average night.

After I brush my teeth, I throw on my running shoes and head to the backyard shed. My shed is roughly ten by ten in dimension, and the roof trusses are just high enough that I can jump rope and do other exercises. There is not much equipment in this shed, only the necessities. This home gym is also not insulated or heated, although I do employ the help of a space heater for those twenty-below January and February mornings. By 4:35 each morning, I throw on classical music or a podcast and begin my workout, usually finishing by 5:15. We have four small children at this point, so I make sure to have my phone ringer on in case my wife needs me to come back inside for any child who wakes unexpectedly.

My workouts usually consist of some weight-loaded movement, a series of bodyweight strength movements, a core movement, and finally a high-intensity cardio exercise. When my workout is finished, I make a pot of coffee, spend about thirty minutes in prayer, and then sit down to write. In fact, the majority of this book was written between 5:30 and 7:00 a.m. Usually, my children sleep until 6:30 or 7:00, and these hours are sacred. I use my writing time to sift through Scripture and the writings of the saints as a time of spiritual reading. Throughout the day, I say a Rosary and various other prayers at different times. When the weather is good enough, I ride my bike to work. This is, however, out of a love for fresh air and not a desire to be "green."

I illustrate this daily routine not to try and make myself look impressive but instead to demonstrate that I am a man who practices what I preach. If I am going to call other men to arms by telling them to make radical life changes, then I had better not be a hypocrite or a phony.

I adopt such a grueling morning routine because I need it to be virtuous. I know that as a man raised in a comfort-obsessed society, I must work against the grain in order to chasten my body and character. There are some people in our culture who still maintain a traditional lifestyle that requires hard physical work and little sleep, like farmers. But for the rest of us, we have grown used to a soft existence. We eat constantly, live in temperature-controlled environments, spend hours in our cars, and view sleep as some sort of idol that must be worshiped. Of course, we need to rest, and I am not suggesting that we arbitrarily give up sleep to do frivolous things. However, if we are to become real hardened men of God, we need to detach ourselves from earthly comforts. How is it that some men in the military are able to thrive off of four to five hours sleep while putting in a day of physically demanding work? The rest of us act as if the sky is falling if we do not get our precious eight hours.

In my opinion, this societal obsession with sleep and self-care is part of a plan the demons have formulated in order to destroy the family. There is no way that a man can sire a large family, provide for the family, and maintain a consistent prayer life if he is concerned with the amount of sleep he gets. There are simply too many things that must be done in a day that a true man must do. Therefore, what an effective method of the devil to insist that we need so much sleep. None of this insistence on prolonged sleep can be found in the Scriptures or lives of the saints. In fact, the Holy Bible is constantly calling us to WAKE UP!

> Thy dead men shall live, my slain shall rise again: **awake**, and give praise, ye that dwell in the dust: for thy dew is the dew of the light: and the land of the giants thou shalt pull down into ruin. (Is. 26:19)

> And Abraham **got up early** in the morning and in the place where he had stood before with the Lord. (Gen. 19:27)

> And **rising early** in the morning, he mustered his soldiers, and went up with the ancients in the front of the army environed with the aid of the fighting men. (Josh. 8:10)

> Yet if thou wilt **arise early** to God, and wilt beseech the Almighty: If thou wilt walk clean and upright, he will presently awake unto thee, and will make the dwelling of thy justice peaceable. (Job 8:5–6)

God is in the midst thereof, it shall not be moved: God will help it in the **morning early**. (Ps. 45:6)

I love them that love me: and they that in the **morning early** watch for me, shall find me. (Prov. 8:17)

Well doth **he rise early** who seeketh good things; but he that seeketh after evil things shall be oppressed by them. (Prov. 11:27)

He that **awaketh early** to seek her, shall not labour: for he shall find her sitting at his door. (Wis. 6:15)

He that feareth the Lord, will receive his discipline: and they that will seek him **early**, shall find a blessing. (Ecclus. 32:18)

And Joseph **rising up from sleep**, did as the angel of the Lord had commanded him, and took unto him his wife. (Mt. 1:24)

And he said to them: Why sleep you? **arise**, pray, lest you enter into temptation. (Lk. 22:46)

These things he said; and after that he said to them: Lazarus our friend sleepeth; but I go that I may **awake** him out of sleep. (Jn. 11:11)

Prooftexting a few Holy Bible verses can be a dangerous game to play when trying to prove a more nuanced point. But the Scriptures are clear on this issue: waking up early to get a running start is a requirement. Of course, there is no commandment that says, "Thou shalt arise with the dawn!" But it is clearly a matter of virtue. We must not fall into legalism as Catholics. This means we need to refrain from looking for ways to avoid what is expected simply because it is not a command. The Scriptures give us many keys to living a virtuous life, and one of the main actions is to wake up early.

Simply put, sleeping is a pleasure, and waking up early is hard. Doing what is hard keeps you from going soft; giving into what is pleasurable and easy makes you soft. Conquer each day from the very beginning by waking up early and as soon as the alarm goes off. It is always tempting to sleep in or press snooze, but do not give in. If you win the first battle of overcoming fatigue, you will have started your day with a victory.

To arise when your eyes are heavy and your legs are stiff is a way that you can train yourself for the resurrection. Sleep is a sort of mini-death we go through to recharge every night, and when we arise through the deadly weight of fatigue, we practice conquering the grave. The old man, the sinful man, wishes to stay asleep and knows not how to escape the grave. Christ showed us the way with his resurrection, and we can pay homage to this every morning.

Some people might object and insist that they need more sleep. Respectfully, if someone is ill and requires rest, then by all means do so. But, contrary to common opinion, I think most of us could stand to do with less. A desire to sleep more is probably a sign that you need to sleep less. We are called to detach from *all* comforts if they can in any manner stand in the way of achieving a life of holiness. Whenever we give God our meagre crusts of bread, he will give us loaves to feed thousands. Give him your sleep in order to chase virtue in the early morning, wait and see what he gives you in return. Our Lord is the Lord of miracles, which means he will give you unexpected grace to persevere. It may be that he multiplies your rest in an inexplicable manner, or he may give you the graces necessary to simply grit your teeth and push through. In either circumstance, you will grow in virtue and in trusting the Lord. Unless you are an early-rising farmer or an eighty-hour per week surgeon, set your alarm at least an hour earlier than you normally do. With this newfound time, you should adopt a new regimen that includes prayer and something physical to start the day, something that chastens the body and hardens your resolve.

Chastening and Mortifying

"He who wishes to find Jesus should seek Him, not in the delights and pleasures of the world, but in mortification of the senses."
—St. Alphonsus Liguori

The word *chastity* comes from the verb *to chasten*, which means "to inflict trouble or pain for the purpose of correction." In essence, chastity calls you to go through a painful reality in order to correct disordered appetites for sexual pleasures. It could be that you need to correct inappropriate desires or that you need to improve your control of healthy desires. We chasten ourselves by living lives that chastise our appetites. When we discipline our children by inflicting unpleasant consequences upon them for their bad actions, for example, we are giving them a chastisement. Hopefully, consequences chasten them in order that they grow in virtue through an acquired understanding of the consequential nature of sinful misbehavior.

St. Paul tells us the following:

For whom the Lord loveth, he chastiseth; and he scourgeth every son whom he receiveth. Persevere under discipline. God dealeth with you as with his sons; for what son is there, whom the father doth not correct? But if you be without chastisement, whereof all are made partakers, then are you bastards, and not sons. Moreover we have had fathers of our flesh, for instructors, and we reverenced them: shall we not much more obey the Father of spirits, and live? And they indeed for a few days, according to their own pleasure, instructed us: but he, for our profit, that we might receive his sanctification. (Heb. 12:6–10)

The meaning of this passage is quite clear: God inflicts corrective pain and punishment on those whom he loves. This means we are called to persevere under discipline and look to God as our Father. Our earthly fathers, in a way, act in the *place of God* when they chastise us. St. Paul ratifies his point with hyperbolic language. He suggests that without receiving chastisement from our fathers, it is as if we are bastards, or fatherless. This could help to explain the epidemic of fatherlessness in our culture. Fatherlessness can take place even in homes where the father is physically present but spiritually or morally absent. At any rate, this chastisement is for our sanctification—to make us holy.

In order to chasten ourselves to accept chastisements from God that lead us to virtue, we need to *mortify the flesh*. In many cases, we could use the words *chasten* and *mortify* interchangeably, but there is a nuance between the two that complement one another. The word *mortify* comes from the word *mors*, which refers to death. This means that *mortification* goes a step further than chastisement.

In the passage quoted at the beginning of this chapter, St. Paul speaks about chastising his body, and he uses the analogy of the athlete who strives for mastery in order to win a race. He reminds us that we show self-control when chasing physical goals. Thus, how much more important is it to chase eternal goals with even more vigor? In his second letter to the Corinthians, St. Paul gives a subsequent addition to his theology of self-mastery: "Always bearing about in our body the mortification of Jesus, that the life also of Jesus may be made manifest in our bodies" (2 Cor. 4:10).

Jesus Christ doesn't receive a personal chastisement, as he is not guilty of any sin; therefore, he has no need of correction for sinful appetites or behavior. In fact, we might even argue that the crucifixion is a supreme chastisement of the human race, as we incur the guilt of deicide (murder of God) through our sin. Paradoxically, this chastisement through deicide is the thing that invites us to be set free through his passion, death, and resurrection. In any case, St. Paul speaks of the *mortification of Jesus* and not the chastisement of Jesus. This is because Christ shows us the purpose of chastening our bodies. St. Paul tells us to *fight* and to bring the body into *subjection* so that we can spread the Gospel of Jesus Christ.

Chastising our bodies gives us the credentials of one who practices what he preaches. And since we are seeking *life* with Christ, we need to continually *die* with Christ, as this is how we obtain eternal life. In a similar manner to sleep being a preparation for death, so too is mortification a preparation for the passion we must go through. Chastising the body is akin to the first step of self-correction. Mortification brings us further from the mastery of the body to the mastery of the soul in order to spiritually participate in a death to self. Dying to self helps us to live out our baptism in which we *die with Christ* so that we can *rise with Christ*.

How Do We Chasten and Mortify?

"Fasting detaches you from this world. Prayer reattaches you to the next world."

—Venerable Fulton J. Sheen

Firstly, it is advisable that you seek spiritual direction before embarking on any significant process of chastening and mortification. It is utterly important that we make a habit of chastening the body so that we can mortify ourselves and share in the life of Christ. Chastening and mortifying ourselves is actually quite simple. You need to partake in difficult activities that help to train your body and passions for holiness. This means that we make daily decisions to forgo certain pleasures and comforts. Also, we make frequent decisions to partake in active moments of physical exertion or discomfort. Here are some examples:

1. Wake up earlier. See the beginning of this chapter.
2. Fasting. Christ tells us that some demons only come out through prayer and *fasting* (see Mt. 17:21). Clearly, fasting is a powerful tool if it drives demons away. Fasting from food helps us to kill the desires of the flesh. This helps with chastity and self-control in other areas, which means we are not as susceptible to temptation. This drives devils crazy, as they have no room to operate on the desires of your flesh, which is their main tactic. There are physical benefits to fasting as well.[1]

---

1   For more on the physical benefits of fasting, go to https://www.meaningofcatholic.com/terrorofdemons/.

3. Physical exertion. St. Paul says, "I so fight, not as
    one beating the air," which means he is not training
    simply to shadow box but instead to punch the dev-
    il in the mouth. We must use St. Paul as the exem-
    plar. We cannot feign virtue or holiness; we have
    to earn it through hard, physical effort. I speak of
    physical exertion rather than strictly working out
    because there are many ways to intentionally train
    our bodies.[2] That being said, we can also train our
    bodies through hard work, like chopping wood or
    shoveling snow. If you already have a physical job,
    there is no need to pile on a weight training sched-
    ule. Instead, seek ways to make certain movements
    physically harder. If you use power tools in your
    job, perhaps use manual tools for some tasks in or-
    der to feel the burn in your forearms and shoulders.
    If you are a farmer, perhaps do the odd task manu-
    ally rather than with a machine if it is appropriate.
    If you have a sedentary job, get a Bluetooth head-
    set and do a conference call while walking, or ride
    your bike to work. Unless you are training for a
    professional sport or to be a Navy Seal, I guarantee
    there is something you can add to your day to chas-
    ten and mortify yourself.
4. Headphone usage. This might sound strange, but
    listening to music and even podcasts or books con-
    stantly on headphones can train our brain to desire
    a constant drip of audible pleasure. It is common

---

2   I have included a training regimen that is adaptable to most
     states in life on the website: https://www.meaningofcatholic.com
     /terrorofdemons/.

to see a young man in sweat pants who is snacking between class, listening to pop music on his earbuds, and sending a message over social media. These things can be a sign of a lack of physical restraint. Music itself can destroy or build a moral compass. Streaming certain music directly into our head at all hours of the day is another way to train ourselves to crave vices for comfort. In fact, exorcists like Father Chad Ripperger require possessed patients to go through a regimen before an exorcism. Throughout the process, all music except for Gregorian chant is cast aside for the duration. It makes you wonder why we should listen to secular music in the first place. There is good non-religious music, like most classical and some traditional folk music. But if you are addicted to music in your headphones, get rid of them.

5. Cold showers. Simply put, cold showers are not enjoyable, and having a cold shower is one of the most unpleasant daily tasks. I learned the value of cold showers while doing a penitential season following the highly recommended Exodus 90 protocol. I do not have ice-cold showers every day, except during Lent and Advent. But I often have at least a cool shower wherein I decrease the temperature as the shower progresses. A hot shower is one of life's greatest comforts. There is no doubt, therefore, that doing the opposite is one of life's greatest discomforts. The old wives' tale of a young man having a cold shower to help with chastity is not really a wives' tale after all. The myth is the idea that a cold

shower on its own will somehow make you chaste. Nevertheless, it is true that consistent cold showers will greatly help you master your body. This will bolster your resolve in avoiding temptations to sins of the flesh. Our Lady at Fatima told the children that more people are burning in hell because of lusts of the flesh than for any other reason. It seems like a good idea that we might seek to *freeze* now rather than *burn* later.

There are numerous other ways to chasten and mortify. Overall, doing something that is physically difficult and that builds virtue is the essence of chastening and mortification. If you tame the horse, you will be capable of heroic and wonderful things. If you let the horse stay wild, he will throw you off and you may break your neck. *Tame the horse*; build cohesion between body and soul.

4

DO NOT REMOVE YOUR SANDALS, YOU STAND ON UNHOLY GROUND

"But if thou forget the Lord thy God, and follow strange gods, and serve and adore them: behold now I foretell thee that thou shalt utterly perish."

—Deuteronomy 8:19

"And they were mingled among the heathens, and learned their works: and served their idols, and it became a stumblingblock to them. And they sacrificed their sons, and their daughters to devils. And they shed innocent blood: the blood of their sons and of their daughters which they sacrificed to the idols of Chanaan. And the land was polluted with blood."

—Psalm 105:35–38

IT is a common trope of modern man to suggest that belief in God is a construct of the imagination. Many believe that materialism or naturalism is more in line with the reality of man. Men who speak like this tend to profess a belief in only things they can see or in things that they can prove. They scoff at the sacred history of the book of Genesis and instead suggest that the origins of man are in some unknown and distant past. According to many, life began in a type of primordial soup rather than in a garden. Yes, we are to believe that an unseen primordial goo is the

53

origin of life. How scientific it is to believe in something that can only be known by faith! This means that the millennia attested history of the Garden of Eden is to many a fairy tale. Perhaps I am just not evolved enough to believe the absurd notion that I should jettison belief in the Holy Bible for a pseudo-creation myth. In any case, modern man has lost his mind. Modern man is insane.

We have all heard the proverbial definition of insanity as doing the same thing over and over again yet expecting a different result. And while this may be an attribute of what an insane man would do, insanity is better defined as a *break with reality*. Insanity entails confusion between truth and illusion or fantasy. Modern man has thrown away the playbook of human history. He has done this in a quest for enlightenment and self-deification.

Our society has forgotten our patrimonial memory of the Fall; thus whole swaths of human beings fall for the devil's tired tactic of telling us that we can be like gods. We worship sex, we worship the natural sciences, and we worship celebrities and politicians. Furthermore, we seek to medicate ourselves out of any redemptive suffering. We sacrifice our children at abortuaries to the gods of prosperity. We murder the sick and elderly as a libation to appease the gods of pain and disease. We advocate for the naturalistic creation myth of the prophet Darwin. Schools look to the pantheon of physicists to tell us the meaning found in a meaningless cosmos. We have replaced the judges of Israel with the black-robed judges of the court. Legal matters are no longer beholden to the law of the Lord but instead to the logic of Lucifer. We look not to God as master of morality but to ourselves.

Occultists are consulted to predict the future, and horoscopes are commonplace. We have recaptured the worship of the sun and moon as lords that rule the day and night. Animals are given human rights while we degrade ourselves to the base nature of the common beast. The cult of the environment has confused people about which heat to fear—they obsess over a slight rise in temperature yet advocate for inhuman solutions that may lead to a place that is burning hot. Our society is godless, Christless, and void of the Virgin Mary. Our culture is no longer Christian; our culture is pagan.

We have given up Roman Catholicism in order to live in pre-Christian Rome. We no longer confess our sins to priests but instead seek validation of our perversions from psychologists. Often, therapy acts as confession without absolution. Even our Church leaders have embraced Muhammadanism as a sister religion. As if Christ the King of heaven and earth could stand in equality with Muhammad the warlord groom of young children. The world tells us that religions are all different at first glance but are the same deep down. The Virgin Mary will not be venerated alongside Vishnu, and Yeshua is not found in the cult of Yoga.

Christendom is dead but, as Hillaire Belloc famously said, "The Faith is Europe and Europe is the Faith." Our Christian civilization was born through death and has been murdered time and time again by Saracen and socialist. Yet, Our Lord is very adept at descending into the dead and calling the dead man to rise. Through the power of the sacraments, we contain the life of Christ within. If we are to recapture our heritage, what rightfully belongs to God, we must rid ourselves and our society of paganism.

Women and Paganism

"To whom then must we make an answer first—to the heretics or to the astrologers? For both come from the serpent, and desire to corrupt the Church's virginity of heart, which she holds in undefiled faith."

—St. Augustine

The next time you stand in line at a coffee shop, take a second and notice what is playing on a screen or look for a woman holding a yoga mat. On the screen, you will likely see a horoscope prediction, and I would be surprised if at least one woman hadn't just come from yoga. Women and men fall for different forms of paganism. Women tend to fall into the more superstitious and overt spiritual forms of paganism. You only need to watch ten minutes of day-time TV to realize that.

It is not only faithless women but also faithful women with weak husbands that are susceptible. Women not rooted in the Faith, of course, do not have any sacramental protection, thus are primed to be victimized. Take a moment to look at the Facebook comments of a given woman on her birthday. You will likely see "light" being sent her way or "wishing good vibes." I imagine that the birthday girl will often "thank the universe." This may seem harmless, but it is not. These practices are superstitious and not based in reality. If someone believes they can send light, then they either believe that natural things are divine or that they have a magical power to control the elements. Of course, many women do not follow the logic out all the way, but more do than you might think. Witchcraft and occult practices are rising exponentially. Even when someone is a generally good person, pagan practices open a door to the demonic. Demons cannot create, but they can manipulate created things. So a woman may look for an uptick in "light" or "energy," and she may receive it from a cursed crystal or yoga. However, this boost will not be from God. Demons love to facilitate immediate gratification, only to drag a sinner to hell for eternal objectification.

Here we will identify a few common pagan traps for women:[1]

1. Yoga. This is a Hindu ritual and is not compatible with Catholicism. Any practice based in a tradition that worships gods is a worship of demons: "For all the gods of the Gentiles are devils: but the Lord made the heavens" (Ps. 95:5). Protestants are wrong in their objection to Catholic statues and art as idols since idols refer to pagan and demonic things. There are numerous other places in the Scriptures that refer to the gods as idols. The Holy Bible is clear: the gods of the pagans are demons. Some will say that they practice yoga merely as a form of exercise. Of course, there are yoga-type movements that are universal to athletics, but this objection is simplistic. If you were to ask a non-Catholic to come to Mass, not as a matter of devotion, but just to kneel and pray and say the responses, this would be a participation in the Faith. Even the idea that you could do something with your body and not affect your soul is dangerous. This is a dualist idea that suggests body and

---

1   I have included an extensive list of popular pagan avenues on https://www.meaningofcatholic.com/terrorofdemons/.

soul are separate things, which is not true. Your soul is the form of your body; hence, what you do with your body will impact your soul and vice versa. Finally, yoga is a divinization process at its root. This means that the participant is called to exalt themselves to the divine nature. This sounds eerily similar to the demon's temptation to *become like gods.*

2. Mindfulness. This is based in Buddhism but dressed up as scientific. It should be noted that there is no way to prove the interior mental health of a person using the natural sciences. Our faith teaches that our soul must be healthy in order for our mind to be healthy. Of course there are certain physical ways to relax or calm down, but none of this can satisfy the needs of the mind. Certainly, none of this can bring you interior peace. Peace is found in Our Lord: "He said therefore to them again: Peace be to you. As the Father hath sent me, I also send you. When he had said this, he breathed on them; and he said to them: Receive ye the Holy Ghost. Whose sins you shall forgive, they are forgiven them; and whose sins you shall retain, they are retained" (Jn. 20:21–23). Peace comes through confession, not mindfulness. If you struggle with interior peace and calm, go to confession and seek holiness. Our Church has a magnificent wealth of spiritual practices that calm the mind and heal the soul. Pick up a Rosary, meditate on the Scriptures, or close your eyes and listen to Gregorian chant instead of practicing mindfulness.

3. Occult practices. These are new age and demonic activities that are clear in seeking the preternatural. Often we call all things spiritual "supernatural" events, but technically speaking, supernatural events are from God. Preternatural things come from the angelic or demonic realm. Occult practices include things like Ouija boards, palm reading, mediums, tarot cards, channeling, witchcraft, and Satanism. Popular shows and music all rely on these things heavily. Harry Potter uses actual spells used by witches, while psychics fool people into believing that the demons with which they speak are instead dead loved ones. Satanism is growing, as are other occult practices, and exorcists are struggling to meet the demand. Men, of course, participate in occult things as well, but there is a strange insistence on priestesses and goddesses in the occult which appeals to women.

4. Superstitious health practices. I am not here speaking about prudential health decisions, or what medicines you do or do not allow yourself or your family. Reasonable minds can differ on things like antibiotics and whether you want to try a natural remedy instead. I am referring to superstitious practices that associate healing power with something inanimate. For example, Chinese medicine is superstitious. Of course, there are herbal remedies that work, but the moment a practitioner reaches for incense and an animal horn, you have entered into a pagan ritual. Also, many mothers swear by little necklaces made of various gemstones that apparently help with

teething. How is this not simply an infant version of healing crystals? It isn't necessary that the object be cursed in order to invite the demonic in the home. As soon as we ascribe active power to an inanimate object, we begin to partake in the sin of superstition, which is ultimately against God. The industries surrounding these superstitious and pagan health methods are rife with occult influence and operators. It is easy as husbands to brush off things in order to appease our wives, but we must stand firm.

Men and Paganism

"The most frequent weak points in man are, from time to time, always the same: pride, money, and lust."

—Fr. Gabriel Amorth, former chief exorcist of Rome

Many pagan activities are common for both men and women, as are most things in life. Yet, there are certain traps that appeal more specifically to men. In the pagan mentality, there is a strong insistence on the divinity or spirituality of natural things. In some cases, men involve themselves in overt pagan and occult practices, like tarot cards or consulting a medium. This is rare, however, as these activities seem to be more for women in the eyes of most men. Unless men find true religion, they tend to view spiritual practices as superstitious, thus they prefer to take a more rationalistic approach. Even when men participate in yoga, they usually insist that it is all about the workout and not the spiritual. Fallen woman most often falls prey to secret hidden spiritual knowledge, like Eve at the Fall. Fallen man most often falls prey to lusts of the flesh and self-worship, like Solomon in the Old Testament. It is worth noting that the entry point is the flesh, but once the door is opened, sinful men are more accepting of obvious pagan spiritualism. Frequently, these traps are brought to them by women who offer sins of the flesh along with dev- ilish practices.

Man cannot help but worship something even if he rejects God. Since modern man tends to disregard spiritual things, this leaves him to worship the creature rather than the Cre- ator. As St. Paul clarifies, self-worship and the worship of created things is the root of sexual deviance: "Who changed the truth of God into a lie; and worshipped and served the creature rather than the Creator, who is blessed for ever. Amen. For this cause God delivered them up to shameful affections. For their women have changed the natural use into that use which is against nature. And, in like manner, the men also, leaving the natural use of the women, have burned in their lusts one towards another, men with men working that which is filthy, and receiving in themselves the recompense which was due to their error" (Rom. 1:25–27).

In this passage from the epistle of St. Paul to the Romans, Paul lays out the roots of pagan practices and the logical moral consequences thereof. In an earlier verse, he speaks of rejection of God leading to idol worship and inevitably to filthy moral activity. This disordered rejection of God results in a disordered moral compass and even disordered sexual appetites. Is it any wonder why there is a veritable explosion of all things LGBTQRS? Our society has so fully embraced paganism that "pride" events take up the entire summer in most cities. Not only are these lifestyles and activities tolerated, but they are also encouraged and seen as virtuous. This is proof of a society that has followed with reckless abandon the creature worship of which St. Paul speaks.

The following areas are ground zero for male oriented paganism:

1. Science worship. In the same way modern man looks to the legal system for moral authority, he also looks to men in lab coats for the meaning of life. There are, of course, legitimate scientific pursuits, but much of today's scientific discourse is pseudo-religious *scientism*—a belief that the natural sciences can provide answers to matters outside their purview. The popular conception of science gives man control over everything from human psychology to material phenomena. For pagan man, the temptation is too great.

2. Evil images. A full chapter on evil images will follow, but it is necessary to include them in this list. Evil images facilitate a worship of self. This may sound strange, but when a man watches porn, he envisions himself in the act. He seeks to watch a version of himself while he commits the sin of self-abuse (masturbation). It is the ultimate act of worship of the creature as the man takes a posture of overseer of his own worship. It is also an inherently homosexual act because the man seeks to pleasure someone of the same sex: himself.

3. Health. Men today are obsessed with their health. Women are as well, but men especially worship the functionality of their bodies. A cursory glance at magazines for men will show the lengths men will go to optimize performance. Sexual performance, mental performance, and athletic performance are the end goal for most men. Ten minutes in a health club is enough to witness dozens of men flexing in mirrors to gaze at their unoriginal tattoos. If you attend a local health club, consider canceling your membership and building a home gym. Gym attire is so scandalous now for men and women that it is inappropriate to spend time in that environment if you wish to stay humble and chaste. Men spend thousands of dollars per year on supplements to achieve pseudo-scientifically "proven" results of a 2 to 5 percent increase in output. It is as if men have returned to the ancient practice of consulting the witch doctor or medicine man for a magic potion that will make them a prince.

4. Money. It is not true that money is the root of all evil; it is the *desire of money* that is the root of all evil (see 1 Tim. 6:10). Men will sacrifice almost anything to the gods of money in today's world. Family size needs to remain small due to money. Marriage is to be delayed and virtue is ignored in a pursuit of the god of cash. With enough money, men feel as if they are masters of their realm, in control of everything. Men have even increased their frequenting of fortune tellers and psychics in hopes of getting an edge in the financial markets.

The amount of occult practice among the highest levels of business is enough for a series of books. In the ancient world, a demon named Baal or Moloch was worshiped. This devil required the sacrifice of children in order to guarantee a successful crop yield. Today, men simply advocate for population control and drop their girlfriends off at the temple of abortion, lest children impede their material progress. Moloch has returned and requires blood.

5. Drugs. It is true that drugs affect men and women. But the combination of self-worship, love of money, science-worship, and health obsession is a potent combination that leads to drug indulgence. More and more men use cannabis as a medicine that apparently cures every illness, mental and physical. University students seek every opportunity to ingest party drugs at electronic music events. This drug-addicted behavior applies to video game dependence and evil images as well. To a man who worships the creation, creature comforts become sacraments he cannot live without. Whole tourist industries now exist to help men fly to the Amazon to partake in psychedelic pagan rituals. Fallen Adam has never learned his lesson as he still flocks to partake in the devil's offering.

These are not exhaustive lists. We could spend dozens of pages identifying more pagan traps that befall the average man and woman. What is most important is finding the most significant items, eradicating them, and living in a state of grace. The faith was born in a pagan world, and all people are pagan until they are baptized. The sacraments and sacramentals are sufficient to defend us and our homes.

Pagan-Proof Your Home

"Even relatively sheltered kids are doing sexual dances without ever having been taught. How is this possible? It is either through learned behavior via the five senses or through some type of cultural osmosis or even by demons that come into the home."

—Fr. David Nix, priest and author

The devils are snakes, and they slither into our gardens in ways that we cannot see. There are important steps we can take to defend our homes and our families from unexpected intruders. Let us look at a few practical ways to take active steps at pagan-proofing our homes.

1. Sanctify your home. Call your local priest and have him come and say exorcism prayers in your home, in each room. A simple house blessing may not be sufficient. It may be that your priest does the actual exorcism prayers in your house during an average house blessing. But in some cases, he may say a generic blessing and splash holy water around. Demons do react to holy water, but if your home still has open doors to the demonic, they will eventually return. Furthermore, make sure the priest says the traditional prayers over the water before using it for a blessing. Technically speaking, blessed water and *exorcised* water may not be the same thing. It can

depend on which prayers are said.[2]

2. Bless your house often with holy water and bless-
    ed salt. You are the head of the household, which
    means you act with priestly authority over your
    domain. Just like in the Tridentine Rite's *Asperg-
    es* ceremony before Holy Mass on Sundays, where
    the entire congregation is sprinkled with holy water
    to renew their baptismal vows, you should cleanse
    your domestic church with exorcised water. You
    can exercise a certain authority over your home
    by using the name of Jesus Christ and various sac-
    ramentals. If you are married with children, I rec-
    ommend you say the following prayers. Sprinkle
    holy water and blessed salt around your house, and
    while you bless your family members with a cross
    of holy water on their foreheads, say: *In the name
    of Jesus Christ I reject any unclean spirits in this
    room, I call on our guardian angels and I call on
    St. Michael to send any demon in here to the foot of
    the Cross to be judged by Jesus Christ.*

3. Purge your house of demonic and pagan content.
    Go through your library and purge anything that is
    against the Faith. The *DaVinci Code, Harry Pot-
    ter*, new age books, many self-help books (many
    use new age principles or atheist psychology), any-
    thing against the Faith must go. It may be that these
    books have been cursed in order to encourage sales.
    The same is true for music and film. Exorcists have

---

2   I have included the prayers on the website, and you can bring them
    to your priest if need be: https://www.meaningofcatholic.com
    /terrorofdemons/.

long attested to the demonic influence on music, and the same is true for film. Exorcist Fr. Ripperger attests to the cursing and hexing of media content in order to encourage sales and attract customers. You gain nothing through secular entertainment, so do not risk your soul.

4. Establish a rightly ordered family life in your home. Men are ordained to be the head of the household. It is not a popular teaching, but it is a central teaching nonetheless. The devil first attacked the headship of the husband in the garden, and he hates a rightly ordered family. Every wife needs to be given the opportunity to stay home with the children. It is the duty of the husband to provide this. This helps your home to become a domestic church. With the wife home more, and the husband providing, children and families are guarded against harmful outside influences. With the consistent female presence in the home, the demons have less room to infiltrate.

5. Control the devices. If you think you can hand a young child an iPad and he will be safe, you need your head examined. If your child is at the age of reason, he can commit a mortal sin. Pornography exposure is common at ages as young as eight. YouTube is full of disgusting content that passes through filters because there is no explicit nudity or swearing. The content is still sexualized and promotes immoral behavior. Think: if you have issues handling a device, how much harder is this for a child? If you hand a child a device without strictly

filtered internet access, you are handing him a loaded gun with mortal sin tipped bullets.

Our society is a pagan wasteland, so we have to take the necessary steps to establish a correct Christian order in our lives. This means that many sacrifices will be necessary. You may have to radically change things in your home and this could cause great backlash from your family. It is better to cause some discomfort now once you recognize that the salvation of your soul and that of your family are at stake.

But before any man reading this supposes himself to be a man worthy of being followed, he must read chapter 7. In that chapter, we discuss how to properly order a home and the characteristics needed for a husband to be worthy of domestic priesthood and submission from his wife. It is not enough to be in charge, as this can easily lead to a dictator-styled tyranny in the home. A wife is required to obey her husband but only in lawful things. Thus, men must sort out their own personal character and virtue before they can expect to be followed.

5

THE DEVIL'S PLAYGROUND

"More souls go to hell because of sins of the flesh than for any other reason."

—Our Lady of Fatima

"I do not hesitate to assert that everyone who has been damned was damned on account of this one vice of sexual impurity (or at least, not without it)."

—St. Alphonsus

HAVE you ever wondered why pornography is free? We pay for everything in life. Food, shelter, entertainment, and even dying costs money. Often it is the things we do for pleasure for which we are willing to pay the most. Think how much you may have spent on vacations. Think of the thousands you may have spent on home theatre systems. Sports equipment does not come cheap, and men will spend more than $70,000 on a pickup truck. All things that we consume in life have a cost—except for these evil images. Sure, there is content that men pay for, DVDs or member-only websites, but the majority is free. There are estimates you can find online that suggest more than 90 percent of porn usage is from free content. Yes, the websites do make money from ads. Yet, it is still mind-boggling from a natural perspective as to why almost all evil images are accessible for free. Imagine if a bar gave away free drinks as a way of getting people into a club with advertisements covering the walls.

People pay for all of their vices, and in many cases, they are willing to go into debt or even commit crime in order to pay. Gamblers spend inherited fortunes, drug addicts shoplift and mug for petty cash. But somehow the most widely distributed drugs on earth—these evil images—are free.

Evil images are free because the devil does not want your money. *He wants your soul!*

Porn is a *get-out-of-heaven-free* card, do not pass Go, do not collect $200. It is a high speed rail system on the rails to perdition. Families are destroyed. Souls are lost. Innocence is taken, minds are perverted, and demons continue to feast. These videos are the devil's magnum opus; he has never had a more powerful weapon. With the click of a mouse or the swipe of a thumb, you give *legions* of devils entrance into your soul and home. A home where the father watches evil images is not a home; *it is a prison.* When a man watches and brings porn into his home, he brings the wrath of God and becomes a plaything to Satan. If you watch porn and die without confession, *you will go to hell.* I understand that some will say I am being uncharitable by emphasizing so strongly on the hellish things. Please hate the messenger all you want as long as you violently remove the infernal intruder out of your home. There is nothing charitable about hell, and there is nothing more serious for men today than the plague of evil images.

How Young Is Too Young?

"But he that shall scandalize one of these little ones that believe in me, it were better for him that a millstone should be hanged about his neck, and that he should be drowned in the depth of the sea."

—St. Matthew 18:6

I was not quite ten years old when I was first exposed to evil images. I remember the day well. It was a Sunday. I know this because as a young boy, my family rarely attended Mass. My whole life I dreaded Sundays, and until I embraced the Faith, I could never understand why. Sunday felt like such an empty day in my soul. Friday was fun, Saturday was great, but Sunday was torturous to my interior life. I know now that my heart longed for God, and the feeling I recall can best be understood as a type of homesickness. I knew this world was not my home, and I wanted to be in my Father's house. It was 1998. I am sure of this because I remember staring at a poster on my wall trying to rid my mind of what I had seen. On the poster were four hockey players who played for team Canada in the Nagano Winter Olympics that year. I stared at NHL hockey players in an attempt to clear my mind and finish the book report due the next day.

Earlier that day, I went to the local college computer lab with a friend from the neighborhood and another man in his early twenties. The man in his twenties was one of our neighbors and was a military veteran. He was a generally upstanding man, and there was no reason not to trust him. My friend was a year older than me and came from a more worldly family. He was the sort of kid who would tell stories of all his escapades to the neighborhood kids. I do not know what happened to him, but I remember years ago hearing he had embraced a less than moral life. I wonder where he is today, and I hope he is happy.

These were the early days of the internet, and it was not uncommon to visit school computer labs to surf the web. Truthfully, there was not much to do for a young kid online then, and most computer activities were still confined to CD-ROM. The older friend who took us to the library had recently received a floppy disk full of pornographic images. I had no idea of this, but apparently the plan was to go to the library and use the computers to check out the pictures. In a way, this was similar to the unfortunate tradition of older males of the household, brothers and even dads, showing their stash of dirty magazines to young boys.

I was almost ten, and my friend was almost eleven. Sadly, kids are exposed to evil images much earlier today in many cases. I was a young man who hit puberty earlier than most, so in theory, I was intrigued by the idea of these images. Of course, I thought women were attractive, and thought it would be fun to see something a little more risqué.

I can tell you that the experience was not what I had expected. Instead of a feeling of carefree excitement, I felt a pang of deep guilt in my stomach. After we returned home in the mid-afternoon, I focused on completing my book report due the next morning. The book I chose was Charles Dickens's *A Christmas Carol*. For years to come, the ghost of that fateful day came back to visit me. My virginal mind was gone, and my innocence was destroyed, naturally speaking. I can recall a Cheerios commercial that I watched later that year. In the commercial, there was an older brother and younger brother sitting and eating cereal together. The older brother was around my age and the younger brother was around six or seven years old. I saw myself in each of the two boys. I looked with sadness at the older boy as I expected he must have been tormented in the same way. And I looked with nostalgia at the younger boy, as I wished to be young and innocent like him again. Not until many years later did I realize the power of confession as the only way to set the interior captive free.

Most men reading this book will relate in some fashion, and I am sure that my story is less tragic than some. But the problem is that my story is common. I see the faces of the young men I encounter when I speak about evil images. A whole room of fourteen-year-old boys could be getting out of hand, but when I speak to them about the danger of evil images, it is as if they have been visited by a ghost. They know it is eating away at their souls, and they are ashamed. As I gaze at my children when they are asleep in their beds, I shudder at the thought of their innocent souls being infiltrated by evil images. I would literally shed my blood to avoid such a horror.

Every child with an internet device in his hand has access to the largest library of hardcore evil images in history. We read about the decadence and revelry of the Ancient Roman Empire. We hear of prostitutes and drunkenness as commonplace. Believe me: the access your son has on the device in his pocket would make Roman revelry look like Sunday school.

Hotel Hell

*"I too have sworn heedlessly and all the time, I have had this
most repulsive and death-dealing habit. I'm telling your graces;
from the moment I began to serve God, and saw what evil there is
in forswearing oneself, I grew very afraid indeed, and out of fear
I applied the brakes to this old, old, habit."*

—St. Augustine

Evil images are the *playground of the damned*. The famous
song *Hotel California* is said to be about the Satanist movement that gained momentum in the 1960s. It is hard to find
mainline information about this, as popular culture cannot
tell the devil from the daylight. But you only need to read
the next few lines from the song to feel the icy chills of the
devil's breath:

> And she said, "We are all just prisoners here, of our own
>   device"
> And in the master's chambers,
> They gathered for the feast
> They stab it with their steely knives,
> But they just cannot kill the beast
> Last thing I remember, I was
> Running for the door
> I had to find the passage back to the place I was before
> "Relax" said the night man,
> "We are programmed to receive.
> You can check out any time you like,
> But you can never leave!"

Using evil images turns a man into a prisoner of his own
device. At the altar of perversion, he gathers together with
millions of people online to the chamber of demons for
a feast of self-worship. Relentlessly, he tries to kill the

dragon, but he just cannot kill the beast. He may try and go back to where he was before, but hotel hell is for reception only. Checking out of this infernal dwelling is humanly impossible, but *nothing is impossible with God.*

If you struggle with evil images, then you need to reread chapter 3 and *crucify your flesh.* An addiction to evil images is more serious than any physical disease. Dying by way of a slow flesh-eating disease would be a better plight than dying a porn addict. I cannot stress this enough: if you die with *one* unconfessed mortal sin, you spend eternity in hell. The following passage is taken from Sister Josefa Menendez's writings. Take to heart the punishments of hell. Think what lies ahead for the souls who die in mortal sin and have lived a life of depravity.

> Then I was dragged along a very dark and lengthy passage, and on all sides resounded terrible cries. On opposite sides of the walls of this narrow corridor were niches out of which poured smoke, though with very little flame, and which emitted an intolerable stench. From these recesses came blaspheming voices, uttering impure words. Some cursed their bodies, others their parents. Others, again reproached themselves with having refused grace, and not avoided what they knew to be sinful. It was a medley of confused screams of rage and despair.
>
> I was dragged through that kind of corridor, which seemed endless. Then I received a violent punch which doubled me in two, and forced me into one of the niches. I felt as if I were being pressed between two burning planks and pierced through and through with scorching needle points. Opposite and beside me souls were blaspheming and cursing me. What caused me most suffering . . . and with which no torture can be compared, was the anguish of my soul to find myself separated from God. . . . It seemed to me that I spent long years in that hell, yet it lasted only six or seven hours. . . . Suddenly I was

violently pulled out of the niche, and I found myself in a dark place; after striking me, the devil disappeared and left me free. . . . How can I describe my feelings on realizing that I was still alive, and could still love God!

I do not know what I am not ready to endure to avoid hell, in spite of my fear of pain. I see clearly that all the sufferings of earth are nothing in comparison with the horror of no longer being able to love, for in that place all breathes hatred and thirst to damn other souls.[1]

Other mystics and saints tell us that the unconfessed sins with which we die will determine the type of punishments we receive if we go to hell. For example, a life of sterilized sexual activity would be punished by life in a sweltering desert with no possibility of quenching thirst. Just like in a contraceptive lifestyle, there is no life in the desert. The garden of the marriage bed becomes a dry wasteland with no hope of any fulfillment or procreation. Porn actresses have a high rate of suicide, and many actresses are underage. If the actress dies, the video is still available online. This means that millions of men have sinned against heaven by pleasuring themselves to the videos of underage dead women. I shudder at the thought of what punishments would fit this crime. Demons do not think like us; they think only in hatred of God. The things they would love to do to us are unspeakable.

Find a good confessor and frequent the sacrament of confession as needed, making a true amendment of life. Receive the graces so that the temptation may go away. Depend on our Lady; keep a rosary in your hand and beg for her intercession every day.

1	Josefa Menendez, *The Way of Divine Love* (Gastonia, NC: TAN Books, 1993).

6

MEDIA MATTERS

"I beseech you therefore, brethren, by the mercy of God, that you present your bodies a living sacrifice, holy, pleasing unto God, your reasonable service. And be not conformed to this world; but be reformed in the newness of your mind, that you may prove what is the good, and the acceptable, and the perfect will of God."

—Romans 12:1–2

"Modern man is staggering and losing his balance because he is being pelted with little pieces of alleged fact."

—G. K. Chesterton

THE average person spends a considerable amount of time in front of a screen in today's world. Of course, not all of this is bad; for example, it took me dozens of hours to write this book. For many activities, screens have taken the place of paper and the time spent on the task is the same. But it is no secret that we spend more time staring at screens for reasons of pleasure and entertainment than ever. There are numerous studies you can read that speak of the dangers of improper screen time. Screen time is not inherently bad, but it must be moderated properly. We simply need to use our common sense to realize that screens can be an issue.

Media is the plural form of the word *medium*, which means a technological method of communication. Books are a form of media, so is the radio and the internet. It is possible to watch good and virtuous things on computers, and it is possible to watch awful things. The same can be said for books. Martin Luther did not need Facebook to effectively cut the Mystical Body of Christ into pieces; the written word sufficed. Not all media forms are created equal, as there can be a qualitative difference among them.

Smartphone screens are engineered to be as pleasing as possible to the eyes of the consumer. This is why people will continually take their phone out of their pocket in order to check if anything has changed. We also know that some technologies do not deliver a given message as effectively as another method. Some people quite enjoy electronic readers; however, many still prefer paper copies of books. MP3 technology has radically changed the transmission and style of music, but music experts agree that vinyl records still facilitate the best sound.

We should be careful with the forms of media we consume; this is certain. However, we must take proactive steps to regulate the content that comes in and out of our minds and homes. Some technologies are better suited for certain actions, but it is not that individual devices or platforms are intrinsically evil. Smartphones have improved the delivery of solid Catholic content via podcasts and e-books but they have also streamlined the deliverance of immoral material. Television can be used to watch *The Passion of the Christ*; it can also be used to binge-watch useless shows, making us like zombies. The content is ultimately the killer; thus, we need to be vigilant and selective of the content that comes into our minds and homes.

In order to regulate the content, we need to differentiate between which forms of media are best suited for different messages. As important as content vigilance is, improper technology usage in general can poke holes in the dam of our resistance to bad content if we aren't prepared.

The Medium Is the Message

"Today the tyrant rules not by club or fist, but disguised as a market researcher, he shepherds his flocks in the ways of utility and comfort."

—Marshall McLuhan

"The medium is the message" is a famous phrase by Catholic Canadian philosopher Marshall McLuhan. In fact, McLuhan was a convert and credited the Blessed Mother with guiding his intellect. He studied media and its effects on people, which led him to his famous expression. He meant that certain forms of media are engineered or best suited for certain messages. Each form of media provides a different platform than another. Different senses are heightened or engaged, and because of this, our minds are in a way tuned to receive things differently.

I mentioned that vinyl records are still preferred by music aficionados. The reason for this is that vinyl records record the physical nature of the soundwaves, and the sound patterns are basically etched into the material. This is why you get a fuller and more complete sound out of a vinyl record. If you have never listened to vinyl, I suggest you do. It is amazing how loud or low the volume can be while at the same time allowing for clear conversations among those in the room. Contrast this with electronic music, which is only enjoyable when played loudly; while at low volume, it has almost no use. Of course, there are exceptions, and I personally know an electronic composer who uses sophisticated technology to make extraordinary music. However, this is because the electronic technology is used to *mimic* the physical sound of live or vinyl music. Essentially, the medium of vinyl records gives us *pure* music and the medium of digital recording gives us *virtual* music. Once again, it is not as if all vinyl music is safe or moral any more than all books are safe or moral. Yet the medium does facilitate a different message delivery, like McLuhan said.

This comparison of different music mediums should give us a guideline for how we distinguish between which media technology we use. We have to take into account the type of behavior associated with each medium. For example, even though you may play the same TV show on different devices, the delivery changes the social bond in the home. If a family sits down to watch a movie together on Sunday night, this is a family activity and all are engaged in something together. If parents give their kids an iPad with the same movie and headphones, this is no longer the same experience. In fact, the content may be irrelevant at this point, as the medium has given the message that isolated enjoyment of media is appropriate.

Internet companies will show happy families in commercials all sitting in the living room on their own devices. The idea is that each person can tailor their choices for themselves. Without having to do any psychological research, imagine the damage this has on a family. Family time becomes a matter of each person enjoying themselves individually. It is just a matter of time before each member of the family isolates himself more often. Also, as a practical measure, it will become extremely difficult to truly monitor the content. Young boys have been finding covert ways to access porn magazines and the like for decades. Even with filters, do you really think you can be in control of what your tech savvy adolescent sees on his own iPad?

Virtue Rot

"The moral virtues, then, are produced in us neither by nature nor against nature. Nature, indeed, prepares in us the ground for their reception, but their complete formation is the product of habit."

—Aristotle

The word *virtue* comes from the Latin word *vir*, which means "man." To be virtuous is to be *manly*. Man was designed to work with his hands; this is why Adam was ordained with tilling the garden. Of course, work, in the sense we know it, is actually a punishment for original sin, but physical cultivation of the soil is part of our nature nonetheless. Leisure is important, and we could actually stand to embrace a better sense of leisure in North America. But laying around watching TV or playing video games for hours is not leisure. When young men lay around in the basement and stare at screens, they are training themselves to be passive. Gazing at a series of Netflix programs for a long period does nothing to engage any higher-order thinking in the viewer. Of course, movies can be wonderful pieces of art, but your average show is designed to keep you addicted or to numb your mind. Furthermore, the very act of laying around slothfully in the middle of the day instead of doing something useful is the opposite of virtuous.

Fallen man suffers from what is called concupiscence. Concupiscence is the disordered lack of self-control that edges us toward sinful behavior. In many cases, this manifests in relatively harmless ways, like eating a little extra cake when we are full. But when we engage in our concupiscible appetites continually, we edge closer and closer to active sin. I personally struggle with overeating. I grew up playing football and developed a typical football diet. I was always lifting weights and getting stronger, so the diet was useful at the time. However, even though I still play sports and exercise, I am older and I have had to work very hard to curb my appetite. For years, I allowed myself to indulge in hearty foods at any given moment, and I run the risk of committing the sin of gluttony if I am not careful. Because eating for pleasure is a physical sensation, this can also weaken my defense against other physical temptations, like drinking and lust. In order to build the virtue to combat gluttony, I have embraced fasting. Without working directly against our vices, we almost always end up falling into mortal sin.

Young hormonal adolescent boys have difficulty with regulating their concupiscible appetites. I have worked with hundreds of teenagers, and even the good ones will still struggle with some vice or another. Most young men struggle with lustful appetites, which is to be expected. In order to fight these appetites, these young men must engage in hard physical activity that requires pain and sacrifice. In fact, Archbishop Fulton Sheen said that maturity means embracing *pain and responsibility.* Allowing a young man to become a couch potato is the exact opposite of this. Kids spend hours at school, an hour or two sitting on the bus, and then hours in front of the TV. It is a recipe for unvirtuous men; it is a recipe for disaster. The virtues of young men who are couch potatoes are like teeth that go unbrushed. For a while, they may hold out, and some may be stronger than others. But, like the teeth, their virtues will rot away. If you or your family have an issue with passive media consumption, something needs to change.

Snakes in the Garden

"Now the serpent was more subtle than any of the beasts of the earth which the Lord God had made."

—Genesis 3:1

Without fail, when I teach Genesis to my students, they ask how the serpent was able to sneak into the Garden. God allowed Lucifer to defect due to pride, which was possible because of his free will. As a result, Lucifer was allowed to tempt Adam and Eve. Without the opportunity to resist temptation, Adam and Eve would not have had liberty to choose virtue. In order to love God, we must learn to love what he loves, and he loves virtue. Even though Adam and Eve were created in a state of innocence, they were not robots, thus they could sin. Somehow, the devil made his way into the Garden of Eden, and the rest is history.

What does this have to do with media? I use this to illustrate how even the best of defenses cannot account for the totality of threats. There is a book called *The Black Swan* written by a former financial trader. In the book, the author lays out a thesis of how unpredictable events are truly that—unpredictable. It is a book written for the mathematically minded, but the thesis is clear: bad things will come at some point and you will not be able to stop them. Some people will also refer to Murphy's Law, which essentially makes the same case.

If the devil can get into the Garden of Eden, he can get through your internet filter. That being said, you *must* enlist the help of passwords and internet filters, even though more is required. With good filters, nothing explicitly pornographic will come through, but there are other dangers. It is not necessary for an explicitly pornographic image to come through, as men have struggled with vices since long before evil images on the internet. St. Paul mentions chastity and condemns lust more than a few times, and that was two thousand years ago. King David saw Bathsheba bathing from afar, and that was enough for him to commit adultery and murder her husband. It is not always necessary to *see* lustful things; it is only necessary for them to be *suggested*.

If your children can send texts, they can receive nude pictures. As a high school teacher, I have seen the damage that sharing sexual content via messaging apps can do to young people. The application Snapchat was designed for sexting.[1]

1   Billy Gallagher, "How Reggie Brown invented Snapchat," *Tech-Crunch*, February 10, 2018, https://techcrunch.com/2018/02/10/the-birth-of-snapchat/.

If you are not familiar with Snapchat, it is an app where users send picture messages that delete after a few seconds. It was designed this way so that messengers could indulge in evil images in spurts without any evidence. Earlier in the book, I spoke of how in the music industry albums and recordings are intentionally hexed in order to encourage sales. I shudder at the idea of how much demonic influence there is over an application designed for young people to secretly watch evil images.

Modern media technologies, including social media and video games, are a part of the culture; email is a necessity, whole industries exist on social media, and video games are a cultural phenomenon. As Catholics, we need not retreat from the world; instead, we must sanctify the world with our actions. Some applications are simply not worth the risk, like Snapchat. But many people have been converted by Twitter recommendations and reading articles posted on Facebook. My wife runs her large Instagram account that focuses on family life and encourages women to serve their families in the home. We need to have *perspective* and *balance* when using the various media technologies. This will look different for most people, as professional rhythms, family obligations, and personal preferences will vary. However, there are a few practical steps we can take to build a healthy usage of media forms.

1. One family computer. There should be one family computer, and it should be in the kitchen or another common area. Of course, if you have multiple school-aged children, you may need a second or even a third computer. However, they must be used

in a common area. There should be no users, at least for your children. No one needs to hide what they are doing online. Be prudent. If you have confidential business documents or financial records, of course, secure your documents if need be. This guideline applies to general computer usage; having a home office or business computer is a different story. Notwithstanding, it builds good habits to use your work device in the common area or with your office door open. Your family will see that how you provide for them is part of the family economy.

2.   One television and no cable. Having one TV means that no one can sneak away to watch a show. It also means that it is harder to get away with watching immoral content. Furthermore, cable services must be cancelled. Recently, I saw a commercial on the Business News Network that was pornographic. Technically, there was no nudity, but it was clearly not geared toward chastity. My children were not paying attention, as the TV was on in the background, but I was horrified. There are no safe channels on TV. How could you expect a culture such as ours to ensure moral content, even on children's channels? If you have cable, you spend upwards of $100.00 per month or more. Sever the connection and instead purchase DVDs or digital episodes of shows you have deemed watchable. Secondhand stores have hundreds of DVDs for sale, and you can peruse online vendors for sales on entire series. You can also purchase sports packages for various professional leagues. You may actually save money

but, most importantly, you may save souls.

3.   Video games. In my opinion, video games are often
      a waste of time, but I do not think they are intrinsi-
      cally immoral. In a world where we spend hours a
      day staring at screens, I cannot for the life of me un-
      derstand why we would also entertain ourselves in
      virtual worlds. However, I understand that playing
      communal games, like racing or sports games, can
      be fun (the virtue of *eutrapelia*, right recreation).
      The same rules for TV and computers apply to vid-
      eo games. They should be on the main television
      in the home. Basement TVs with video games are
      a colossal mistake. Basement video game setups
      are an invitation to you and your children to be-
      come a Mountain Dew addicted waste-case. Most
      young people have no real virtue or defense against
      overindulgence. Video games are engineered to
      spike dopamine levels in your brain and give sim-
      ilar highs as things like cocaine. You must be very
      careful, and I would recommend little to no video
      game usage in the home unless you are certain your
      kids are morally formed.

4.   Inspect all books. Books have led many souls to
      hell. There is a saying in traditional seminaries
      that you need to ask your superior for permission
      to do anything, even to go to hell. This is a ref-
      erence to the section in the library that contains
      books by heretics, bad philosophers, and those of
      other religions. For certain reasons, it may be the
      case that a seminarian needs to read about Muham-
      madanism or Martin Luther. However, the superior

only allows this with caution and oversight so as not to expose the seminarian to attractive yet damnable ideas. If a seminarian needs protection, how much more do your kids need? This also applies to schooling. If you cannot ensure good books in your kids' school, you need to seek alternatives, which may even mean homeschooling, something I highly recommend.

Do What Is Necessary

"You know the affliction wherein we are, because Jerusalem is desolate, and the gates thereof are consumed with fire: come, and let us build up the walls of Jerusalem, and let us be no longer a reproach."

—2 Esdras 2:17

There is a story from Christendom about a village that was inundated with sinful behavior. The villagers seldom fulfilled their religious duties, and the tavern and brothel were full. An exorcist was called to help, and when he arrived, he saw a surprising scene. Expecting to see a host of demonic warfare, instead he saw demons lazily taking naps and barely tempting. The villagers had already given in, and the demons had nothing to do. The exorcist then visited the village down the road full of holy men and women and found a different scene. In this town, the demons were working on overdrive, in constant conflict with the guardian angels and intercession of the saints. The piety of the village people in the holy village necessitated voracious efforts from the devils. But even with all these attacks, the villagers were formed in virtue and continued to triumph.

Your home must be the second village, which means you have to work hard to keep the demons away. If a devil can use an unwitting friend of your child to send a suggestive text or song, he will.

There is an appropriate age when young people can handle a relative amount of temptation, but it is not until they have formed a strong character. If your child has grown up with a device always in hand, I fear you may have to take drastic measures. If you truly love your children, you will take the necessary steps to remove from them the internet and video game devices that are the source of overindulgence. This may mean tantrums, but it is better for your teen to tantrum than for the tempter to triumph. Once your children consistently demonstrate good decision-making skills and a strong conscience, only then can you extend to them personal device time. You cannot expect to have a garden free from all snakes, so your children need to become expert snake killers before you expose them. Furthermore, all of this information may well apply to you. If you cannot demonstrate virtuous media behavior, what can your family and peers emulate?

Depend on Our Lady's intercession to help you protect your family from the serpent. I like to imagine she crushed the head of the serpent in snake-skin boots. Let the Virgin loose in your home; she knows what she is doing.

7

BUILDING A DOMESTIC CHURCH

"But if it seem evil to you to serve the Lord, you have your choice: choose this day that which pleaseth you, whom you would rather serve, whether the gods which your fathers served in Mesopotamia, or the gods of the Amorrhites, in whose land you dwell: but as for me and my house we will serve the Lord."

—Josue 24:15

"Being men, we sin every day, but St. Paul consoles us by saying 'renew yourselves' from day to day. This is what we do with houses: we are constantly repairing them as they break down. You should do the same thing to yourself."

—St. John Chrysostom

BEFORE I embraced the Catholic faith, I was very much *of the world*. I was not an ax murderer, but I certainly was not close to a saint. When I speak about my conversion to people, I am usually asked what kind of man I was. I answer very simply: I was like everybody else. I mean that I followed the world's playbook. I very rarely went to church. I fell for the whims of worldly philosophies, and I lived in a constant state of mortal sin. Stop for a moment and think about how often you see your neighbors coming out of the confessional. Now, think about how common it is to use evil images, to party, to fornicate, to

91

take the Lord's name in vain, and to miss Holy Mass. Historically, there have been saints who have lived a life without committing a mortal sin, although this is statistically unheard of. Many people you interact with on a daily basis are living in a state of mortal sin.

Why is this important? Sin, both venial and mortal, can contribute to a darkening of the intellect; mortal sin is especially dangerous in this regard. This means that living a life without sanctifying grace literally affects your intelligence. Put in layman's terms: sin makes you stupid.

If you live by the rules the world presents, you will live by stupid rules. We live in a time of great material abundance, yet both men and women are increasingly unhappy. So-called sexual liberation has led to contraception, adultery, divorce, and destroying unborn children. A large rejection of the teachings of the Catholic Church has led to a blind obedience to political correctness and the state. The average person thinks we have progressed, yet we can no longer handle basic human relationships like marriage.

In the past, you were expected to save yourself for marriage, fall in love, get married, then have children. Most were married in their late teens or early twenties. It may be hard to imagine now, but people recorded a much higher level of happiness even seventy years ago. Life may have lacked as much material comfort, but it did not lack meaning and order. Today, people are expected to commit fornication to find out if they like someone. Then they may move in together, and perhaps they will buy a house. If they think it is the right time, they may have one or two children, after which they promptly spay and neuter themselves like animals. At some point, they may get married, unless they have already separated. The traditional and sane order of life is literally upside down.

In most homes, both mom and dad spend nine to eleven hours away from the house if you account for an average work day and travel time. As soon as mom returns to work after maternity leave, the children will spend the majority of their lives being raised by someone else. On top of this, children spend even more time away from their parents in lessons and sports. The most important thing we can do as men is to get our families and ourselves to heaven. Yet we seem to do everything we can to ensure that our family is raised by someone else. Our society cares nothing about the moral health of you and your family, and you will have to work tirelessly and against the grain.

Once Upon a Time

"What is called matriarchy is simply moral anarchy, in which the mother alone remains fixed because all the fathers are fugitive and irresponsible."

—G. K. Chesterton

Once upon a time, it was common to hear the church bells ring at morning, noon, and night. Throughout all Catholic populations, men, women, and children would stop to pray the Angelus. Three times per day, the average Catholic thought of Our Lady and the incarnation of her Son. Families went to Mass multiple times per week, and fasting norms were much more vigorous. That being said, it wasn't just fasting and Mass attendance that were more common, feasting and merriment were common as well.

Catholics lived a life filled with the rhythms of the Church's calendar and, although things were not perfect, people were happier with less. Men worked hard, wives tended to beautiful homes that truly were deserving of the term "domestic church." When men went to work, they went to work for their wives, their children, and their God. Men provided for their families, and children looked to their fathers with admiration. Men lived to serve their wives, and wives lived to serve their husbands. The family name meant something, and wives took the name of their husband without question.

We spoke at length about effeminacy and the roles of men and women in an earlier chapter, but it is worth revisiting this topic for a moment. Men and women have roles designed by God that are reiterated through the natural law. It is disordered for women to be the head of the household because men are priests by nature. Think about a parish where the priest is lacking in masculine virtue. I would imagine that the preaching is weak and the liturgy is bland. Do you see female altar boys serving at Mass? Are the majority of the readers women? Does anything in the parish evoke a sense of masculine service and strength when you enter?

I am not blaming women per se, just as I am not blaming men per se. But whoever is to blame, our homes and our parishes are in a state of disorder. It is not that women aren't capable of doing most things that men can do, and the opposite is also true. However, men and women were designed for a different purpose. Think for a moment about the most common professions for the average working woman. Most women work in nursing, education, human resources, and social services. When women leave the home, they cannot help but seek a job in which they are mothering for a living. Now think about the most common professions for men. In most cases, you will find men gravitating toward leadership positions or jobs that require technical skills, whether physical or mathematical. If you were to think of the most unhappy man you know, I would imagine he works a sedentary job and has no opportunity to exercise leadership over anyone. Most likely he does not show any leadership in the home either. Like most men, he has bought into the lie of equality.

There is no equality between the sexes. This is not because each does not share equal dignity, which is clear as we are both made in the image and likeness of God. There is no equality because we are not equals. To be equal means to be the same, and men and women are not the same. Try to think of how you could show equality between men and women. Is there a way to do it without splitting things half-and-half between them? Would anyone say there is equality in a home if the husband works and the wife takes care of the home? Of course not. The concept of egalitarianism is inherently evil because it is not how God ordained the relationship between the sexes. Man was made to have dominion, and woman was made to help him. This does not demote woman to a secondary role; rather, it promotes man to a level necessitating heroic responsibility. God created each of us with a nature, and in the same way you cannot domesticate a wild animal, you cannot force men and women into equal roles. The results will be what they have been: divorce, perversion, sexual immorality, broken homes, and ultimately depression and suicide.

Classic gender roles are not easy; in fact, they require so much more than modern gender expectations. Being a sole provider is much harder for a man than if his wife were to work as well. Staying home with any number of small children is much harder than going to work. Colleagues of mine constantly tell me that my wife "must be tough" to be home with all those kids. Or they say to me, "How do you guys afford everything?" I am going to let you in on a little secret: if you follow God's plan for marriage, things will work out. What a novel concept! Imagine, following God's will results in happy and fruitful marriages.

Before you begin to see even a semblance of a thriving domestic church in your home, you must sort out the role of priest. You are not doing any service to your family if you seek equality, and just like parishes led by weak pastors, your congregation will suffer.

Out of Egypt

"And Moses said to the people: Remember this day in which you came forth out of Egypt, and out of the house of bondage, for with a strong hand hath the Lord brought you forth out of this place."

—Exodus 13:3

Leading your family as the priest of the home is not a simple task. Getting your own spiritual and moral life in order is hard enough. If you are a single man reading this, it still applies to you. We all need to escape from the bondage that our culture offers us, whether we are married or not.

Due to our fallen nature, we tend to rebel; for evidence of this, see the Old Testament. For thousands of years, it is a similar story over and over again. Even the Israelites who walked across the Red Sea did not take long to rebel against the priestly command of Moses. In some cases, your family will take to your household priesthood, but often you will encounter resistance. It is futile to try and force your family to accept the proper order of things all at once. Moses parted the Red Sea and performed the greatest of wonders, yet his spiritual children still rebelled.

If you have long lived a worldly life with disorder in the fabric of your home, it will be humanly impossible for you to right the ship. I say *humanly impossible*, but not impossible with God's guidance. When Moses went up the mountain to receive the Ten Commandments, we read in the Holy Bible that the people "rose up to play" (Ex. 32:6). This is biblical terminology that means they engaged in sexually deviant behavior and ritual debauchery. They had come out of a pagan culture, and pagan religious rituals were always mixed with ritualistic sexual practices. It would have been a scandalous scene.

Contrast the two main priests: Moses and Aaron. Aaron, of course, overall is a great hero of the Old Testament. But even he falls into this carnal ritualism as he performs priestly functions with the golden calf. On the other hand, Moses is hardened and stoic in his priesthood and casts out immorality and rebellion with severity. What is so different about Aaron and Moses? It is probable that Aaron, a slave, grew up with at least a semblance of the old traditions from Abraham. Whereas Moses, a prince, was steeped in Egyptian paganism in the royal court. The difference between the two is that Aaron, although an Israelite, left Egypt, but Egypt *had not* left him. Moses, although raised pagan, had spent years in the desert before he began to liberate his people. We read that Moses was away from Egypt for "a long time" (Ex. 2:23) and that he finally met the Lord in the "inner parts of the desert" (Ex. 3:1). The major difference between Moses and Aaron is that not only had Moses left Egypt, but he made sure *Egypt had left his soul.*

In an ideal situation, we should be raised in a faithful family, void of paganism and immorality. But this is often not the case, even in Catholic families. The Israelites of Egypt had mingled so much of the Egyptian paganism with their traditions that in many cases it would have been hard to distinguish. If you refer back to chapter 4, you will recall the prevalence of paganism in our lives today. Practicing Catholics are still going to psychics to "talk" with dead loved ones, for example. When a psychic "communicates" with a dead loved one, he is either a fraud or he is communicating with a demon pretending to be your loved one.

Just like the Israelites who were in Egypt, so many of us still cling to the Egypt in our souls. In order to become the domestic priests we are called to be, we need to follow Moses's example and spend time in the desert. If you are a bachelor, this will be much easier for you. If you are married with children, then you will have to find creative ways to bring the desert into your home.

Keep Egypt Out of You: Rule of Life

"And the Lord spoke to Moses, saying: Go, get thee down: thy people, which thou hast brought out of the land of Egypt, hath sinned."

—Exodus 32:7

In order to rid your soul of Egypt, you must practice asceticism. In chapter 3, we laid the foundation for taming the horse based on mortification and chastening of the body and will. In chapters 4, 5, and 6, we identified the trappings of paganism, evil images, and other media forms. With the help of that information, it is now time to form a rule of life. A rule of life is in essence a routine or schedule that helps facilitate spiritual and moral success in your vocation. Traditionally, religious orders take vows and follow a strict rule of life. Famously, the *Rule of St. Benedict* is followed by various monastic traditions. Everything from diet to prayer time, prayer method, study, and recreation is outlined in the rule of life. Good seminaries ensure their candidates follow a sound rule, and there are also lay orders of non-consecrated people that follow a rule.

It is important to think in terms of a rule rather than a simple schedule. The reason for this is that schedules can be interrupted for all sorts of reasons. If you are a married man, children and family duties can bring untimely interruptions. Even if you are a priest or bachelor, a man truly devoted to God will be devoted to others as well, which means your time will not always be your own. If people depend on you, then you will be called to action in ways that conflict with your schedule. In fact, I often find that men who insist on commitment to a personal schedule are among the most selfish men I know. The schedule for many men becomes an idol, something to worship. Sleep patterns must be kept, meals must be prepped for strict diet and exercise. Alone time is required, and they cannot overcommit themselves. We are called to be *other Christs*, which means we are called to self-sacrifice through the cross. We are called to empty ourselves for the love of God and neighbor. We are ultimately called to be *crucified*.

That being said, Jesus did live by a rule of life. First, he lived by the Law of Moses, as he was faithful to the precepts of the Old Covenant. But he demonstrated to us that there is a *spirit of the law* as well as a *letter of the law*. This means that all laws are ordained with a purpose. For example, the first commandment requires us to put God above all. Yet this commandment requires obedience to God's will as a first principle. Therefore, if we were to neglect our fatherly duties and use prayer time as an excuse, we would be mistaken. The letter of the law is that God comes first, the spirit of the law requires that God's will takes primacy. God does not will us to neglect our family in order to finish a grueling prayer regimen, although in the best case we will have a strong prayer life that nourishes our vocation. We live by a rule of life rather than a schedule of life because following God's commandments requires adherence to both the spirit and the letter.

When Christ heals a man on the Sabbath, the Pharisees protest that he should not be healing on a holy day, as it is a form of work. Christ responds, "Which of you shall have an ass or an ox fall into a pit, and will not immediately draw him out, on the sabbath day?" (Lk. 14:5). In the strict sense, healing is a type of work that is forbidden on the Sabbath. But Christ makes the distinction between servile or unnecessary work and work geared toward the necessary good of the person or animal. For example, a farmer cannot refuse to do chores on Sunday, as his animals would suffer. Yet, he can refuse to sell his product or purchase equipment, as it can be done the next day.

This should give us context for how we formulate our personal rule of life. Here are some things to consider when putting together your rule:[1]

1. It has to be doable. When I first began to take a rule of life seriously, I had dreams of saying loads of prayers and constantly fasting and mortifying myself. As I write this, I am the father of four children under four years old. For a short time, I was able to accomplish an unrealistic prayer and mortification regimen, but it was unsustainable. This book is written to challenge men, and I am not advocating for an easy rule. Nevertheless, we are called to *finish the race*, not run as fast as we can out of the gate. Your rule should be challenging but not unrealistic. Over time, you will become stronger, and through the graces bestowed by God for your efforts, eventually you will have a rule that rivals anyone's.

2. It has to amplify your life, not detract from it. If you are a bachelor, then your rule should be geared toward maintaining your chastity and preparing

---

1   On the website, there is a template that you can use and adapt to your needs: https://www.meaningofcatholic.com/terrorofdemons/.

for leadership in marriage. If you are a father, then your rule should make you a better husband and parent. I know I function better with early morning exercise, and I cannot take time away from daily obligations to write in most cases. Thus, my rule requires a 4:30 a.m. wake-up. I say a morning offering or St. Michael Prayer, pray the Rosary, and read the Holy Bible or do some spiritual reading or study throughout the day. I fast often and maintain the meatless Friday tradition. Traditionally, Catholics fasted and abstained from meat on every Friday of the year, except if there was an exception for a particular feast. The current code of Canon Law allows for an episcopal conference to substitute another act of penance instead of abstaining from meat. Canon 1251 says that unless it has been stipulated by the hierarchy, abstinence from meat or some other food is to be observed on each Friday of the year. Canon 1253 states that a given conference of bishops could determine other ways for Catholics to do penance on Fridays. Personally, I cannot think of a way that my conference of bishops has clarified any other form of penance that fits this description. For mortification, I have cool or cold showers and generally do not eat between meals. All of this keeps me sharp, and peppering my day with little sacrifices keeps me focused on God. If I did less, I would be selling myself short, and if I did more, I would overextend. My prayer life will continue to develop and, one day, I will do more. The point is to find the same balance for yourself so that you can challenge yourself but also fulfill the duties of your state in life.

3. It should not become stagnant. It is a good thing to cultivate habits, and we should not expect the Holy Ghost to descend in the form of a dove every time we say the Rosary. Yet, we need to have variety in order to keep ourselves sharp. The Church has always had fasts and feasts. This not only sharpens our understanding of the liturgical year but also stops us from getting overly accustomed to a way of living. If cold showers become normative and are no longer as difficult, then go back to warm ones and shock yourself again with cold. Adapting to a meatless diet would nullify the difficulty of Fridays. Keep the framework the same, but tweak things here and there to keep yourself guessing. Add devotions for different seasons, and really celebrate the major feasts. Join large novena prayer movements that can be found online and participate in the Church's indulgences. Keep your life Catholic from dawn till dusk and have fun with the Faith. Being a Catholic is a serious thing, but it is also an amazing way to be truly happy, even through suffering.

Your domestic church requires your unyielding service as the priest of the home. Whatever your situation, a greater spiritual formation through a rule of life will only improve things over time. You may be married to a faithful woman, you may not. This may be the first Catholic book you have read. Perhaps you are in the seminary or preparing for marriage. No matter your state in life, you are called to priestly duties in some capacity. A faithless wife will not be won over by argument alone. Your unruly children will not be convinced of the Faith by gimmicky music and watered-down liturgy. You will never become a priest worthy of martyrdom if you seek to be admired and comfortable. Only a heroic man will suffice for a civilization as depraved as ours. Only a man cut from diamond, a man who lives by a rule, will finish this race. Cultivate your garden into a church worthy of Christ and you will become a man worthy of Christ's Church.

8

CAMEL KNEES

"It's impossible to lose your footing when you're on your knees."
—Venerable Fulton J. Sheen

"Pray without ceasing."
—1 Thessalonians 5:17

IN the book *Church History* by the ancient historian Eusebius of Caesarea, we read of St. James the Apostle. In his account of the martyrdom of James, Eusebius relays the following about St. James's prayer life: "He was in the habit of entering alone into the temple, and was frequently found upon his knees begging forgiveness for the people, so that his knees became hard like those of a camel, in consequence of his constantly bending them in his worship of God." This account from Eusebius comes from the early 300s, and he references an even earlier source. Thus we have no reason to doubt this claim. Furthermore, Eusebius mentions this as if it was a known fact about St. James. St. James spent so much time on his knees begging for forgiveness for the people of Jerusalem that he had camel knees. I have seen men with hardened knees from prayer. I cannot imagine the amount of time it would take to develop knees as knobby and hardened as a camel's. This would mean hours every day, on a hard surface, no kneelers, no breaks.

It is probable that St. James engaged in some spontaneous and freestyle prayer. Due to his proximity to Jesus and his incredible holiness, I am sure he reached the heights of prayer. His life would have consisted of the miraculous and the mystical. Nevertheless, he was raised a pious Jew, which meant he would have been raised in the prayer tradition of ancient Hebrews.

It is a common misconception among Protestants that the Early Church resembled a Bible study or praise and worship gathering. Due to the infiltration of poor scholarship and Protestantism into the Church, even educated Catholics hold on to ideas about an early Church that never existed. The early Church was distinctly Hebraic, which is why Peter and Paul had a sharp confrontation about the Law of Moses in the New Covenant of the Catholic Church (see Gal. 2). Ancient Judaism of the Old Covenant was much more like Catholicism than modern Rabbinic Judaism. Synagogues were liturgically based and much more resembled a traditional Catholic parish. Ritual baths were common as a sort of precursor to baptism. The faithful would even confess their sins secretly to the high priest, who transferred them to the sacrificial lamb or goat. The priests wore majestic vestments, and the Temple of Jerusalem was home to actual blood sacrifice and magnificent liturgy. The ancient Catholic Mass barely resembled the modern Mass and is better represented in the ancient liturgies of Eastern Catholic Churches and traditional Latin parishes. In any case, the early Church was not a protestantized praise and worship centered "faith community." It was a ritualist, sacramental, liturgically centered *Catholic Church*. This was the context for the camel knees of James.

Recipe for Success

"Wherefore being desirous that this nation also should be at rest, we have ordained and decreed, that the temple should be restored to them, and that they may live according to the custom of their ancestors."

—2 Machabees 11:25

My Nonno and Nonna, God rest their souls, came to Canada in 1967 with my mother and her siblings. I was raised in an Italian atmosphere and lived in Italy for a time as a young man. As you can imagine, I developed a great love for Italian food, especially that of my Nonna. My family is from a small village called Vorno outside of the city of Lucca, nestled in the heart of Tuscany. When I lived in my mother's childhood village, I witnessed firsthand the ancient culinary traditions passed down through the generations. In North America, we are so caught up with change and development. We hold to the idea that things need to be constant in their improvement in order to be relevant. Technology must be updated frequently, new models of cars are produced, and every politician has a new vision. Italy is an ancient culture, and even through a radical decline in the practice of the Catholic faith, the rhythms of the nation still reverberate from the past. In fact, in most cases, even urban and progressive-minded Italians tend to be resistant to foreign food. There are, of course, various ethnic restaurants to serve immigrant populations, but Italians eat Italian food. Full stop.

Every Italian has a Nonna, which means every Italian knows who makes the best spaghetti, lasagna, risotto, or tiramisu. Some recipes are simply perfect. There is nothing you can do to improve your Nonna's chicken cacciatore. In fact, I might argue that trying to change her recipe would be a sort of culinary sacrilege. I have always had an affinity for cooking and eating, and I tried for years to recreate my Nonna's *sugo*—her meat sauce. Never was I able to recreate her legendary sugo until I spent the time to learn to cook exactly as she did. Every spice, every vegetable, even the temperature in the pot had to be the same. If I really wanted to eat Nonna's sugo, then I had to cook it her way.

I make this sauce frequently and it is the same every time. This consistency in operation does not take away from the experience but instead brings me back to my Nonna's kitchen. Every time I hear the crackling sound of beef and sausage touching the oil, I hear my Nonna. When I smell the vegetables and herbs permeate the kitchen, I smell every Christmas feast at her crowded table. This recipe I inherited from my Nonna is not a mere formula for food, it is a tradition of love and devotion. In every action of cooking her sugo, my Nonna is present in a mysterious manner as I work away. By recreating her life's work over and over again, I show her how much I still love her, even if she is gone. If I truly love my Nonna, out of reverence and humility, I will do as she taught me. To deviate from her ways would, in a way, be disrespectful. This same logic should apply to our prayers and devotions, as our ancestors in the Faith have also given us perfect recipes to follow.

Pray Like a Saint

"My little children, your hearts are small, but prayer stretches them and makes them capable of loving God. Through prayer we receive a foretaste of heaven and something of paradise comes down upon us. Prayer never leaves us without sweetness. It is honey that flows into the souls and makes all things sweet. When we pray properly, sorrows disappear like snow before the sun."

—St. John Vianney

If we are to develop a prayer life like Ol' Camel-Knees St. James, we need to know how to pray. As Catholics, we have inherited a magnificent tradition of spiritual resources. Yet for many, it is difficult to cultivate a prayer life. The infection of Protestant theology into the Church has left the impression that prayer is best when it "comes from the heart." Of course, we want our prayer to be heartfelt, but that does not mean we have to always pray spontaneously or differently. In fact, the desire for prayers to come from the heart should be fueled by our love for God and the saints. In the same way that I show my Nonna unyielding love in following her recipe, we show God our hearts by imitating the saints in prayer.

The saints are very special to God, and he uses them as instruments to show the world the Gospel. There is a diversity in how the saints pray, but it is a *symphonic diversity*. All the saints pray in ways that are similar to other saints. For example, the Rosary as we know it comes to us just over a thousand years after Christ. Nevertheless, devotion to the Blessed Mother can be seen in the earliest devotions and hymns of the Church. The Rosary became such a staple in the prayer life of Catholics because it provided a way to formulaically pray what was always believed. The saints were holy; therefore, out of humility and piety, they sought to continue the traditions handed to them. St. Paul says to "hold fast to the traditions" (2 Thess. 2:15), and thus we should seek to pray in the same traditions as the saints.

One of the objections that Protestants level against Catholics is that we practice what our Lord calls "vain repetition" (Mt. 6:7). Unfortunately for the Protestant, this is a misunderstanding of what Christ means. Christ here is referring to chanting of meaningless phrases put on for the sake of showmanship, pagan or otherwise. Christ is the eternal Priest, and because of this, he presides over the eternal liturgy. In the Old Covenant and the New Covenant, the liturgical function of a priest always requires formulaic repetitions of powerful prayers. In the Temple of the Jews, there was a constant recitation of the Psalms, and certain liturgies required the same prayers to be said every time. The same is true in the Holy Sacrifice of the Mass. Regrettably in the New Mass, the priest is given options to choose between or even omit certain prayers. Traditionally, however, the exact same prayers are said day in and day out by Catholic priests. Furthermore, Our Lord tells us to pray the Our Father. If Christ taught that the repetition of prayers was in vain, then he would be instructing us to sin. This is, of course, nonsensical. Also, Protestants are famous for repeating certain verses of the Holy Bible ad nauseam. The bulk of the Hail Mary is directly from Scripture; therefore, repetition of the Hail Mary is akin to the repetition of Scripture.

There is nothing wrong with praying the same prayers often, just as there is nothing wrong with frequently practicing your golf swing. If you want to master an art, you must practice that art repeatedly. The same is true with prayer. Praying the Our Father many times a day only reiterates your desire for God's will to be done. Since you and I fail at doing God's will, it is advisable to pray another Our Father. Christ gives us his mother to love as our own. If we wish to grow closer to the Blessed Mother, then we should be continuous in approaching her in prayer. We have received perfected prayers from the Holy Bible and the saints over the centuries, and we should make them the focal point of our lives.

You can never pray enough of these prayers: Our Father, Hail Mary, Glory Be, Guardian Angel Prayer, Salve Regina, or St. Michael Prayer.[1]

The Purpose of Prayer

"Theological insights are gained not only from between two covers of a book, but from two bent knees before an altar."

—Venerable Fulton J. Sheen

There was a woman known for being a fiery anti-Catholic who was close to finishing post-graduate studies in theology. She may have harbored animosity toward the one true Faith, but this was because she sought to love God. She thought Catholicism was wrong; therefore, she believed the Church to be against the will of God. She was an honest intellectual, so she began to investigate the writings of the early Church Fathers. Like many converts before her, she

---

1 See the website for an extensive list of traditional prayers: https ://www.meaningofcatholic.com/terrorofdemons/.

found that the early Church was distinctly Catholic. She found a Church full of sacraments, Marian devotion, priests, and bishops. As you may imagine, she was perplexed and troubled at her findings. She had made her living up till that point as an anti-Catholic preacher and now faced a crisis. She loved our Lord Jesus but, like all of us, was attached to worldly comforts. She had to decide between continuing as a Protestant and risking losing everything to become Catholic.

One day, she decided to visit a Catholic church. She was so nervous about being seen at a Roman church that she traveled far from town to a country parish. This event took place before most parishes were gutted after the Second Vatican Council. The little parish still maintained its traditional beauty, inside and out. She arrived at 7:00 a.m., much earlier than the 8:30 a.m. Mass. She needed to work up the nerve to enter the church, and she figured she could take a look around and perhaps ask some questions before the congregation arrived. She sat in her car, nervous and conflicted.

She saw a father and his daughter walk into the church shortly after she arrived. Protestant churches aren't even churches in the strict sense. There is no altar or sanctity to the building; therefore, people rarely spend time in the worship space outside of the service. But a father and his daughter arrived over an hour before Mass. She waited a few more minutes, expecting the father and daughter to come out. Yet, they did not.

Within a minute or two, another young woman walked into the church. The Protestant woman decided it was time to enter the parish before others arrived. She had never been in a Catholic church and did not know what to expect. As she entered the church, she was stunned. She was shocked by the beauty of the murals, architecture, and statues. The high altar seemed to reach endlessly to heaven. The precise detail of the stained-glass was overwhelming. It was as if she had entered *heaven* on *earth*. When she regained her wits, she looked for the father and his daughter. She found them kneeling side-by-side as the father led his beautiful young daughter in the Most Holy Rosary. Both father and daughter prayed quietly and reverently with their eyes closed as their fingers caressed the beads. It seemed to her like the most natural scene she had ever seen, a father leading his daughter in prayer to Our Lady.

Finally, she caught a glimpse of the young woman who had entered the church shortly after the father and daughter. This young woman was gracefully moving about the church as she contemplated the icons. At each image, she would bow her head, place her hand on the image, and say quiet prayers to herself. It was as if she was floating between each picture without touching the ground. Suddenly, the Protestant woman began to weep. She fell to her knees and placed her head in her hands. It was clear to her that all the theological training in the world could not teach her a fraction of what the young woman knew from contemplating the icons. She loved Our Lord, and she wanted to know him better. Her pride was shattered, her defenses were lowered. She was brought home to the Catholic Church by the quiet prayers of a humble woman. She eventually joined a religious order and lived her life as a prayerful nun.

Prayer is a gift from Our Lord that we use to come to know him better. There are high-minded theological aspects to the spiritual life, and there are various techniques. But in the end, we pray because we want to know God.

When we kneel, we kneel before the King. When we cross ourselves, we mark ourselves with the death of Christ. When we clasp our hands together, we hold on to the divine life. When we recite the words of our prayer, we cast all our worries and pains on his mighty shoulders. If we want to be Catholic men, then we must be men of prayer. Our souls need prayer more desperately than our bodies need food. In the end, the purpose of prayer is to bring us closer to the Lord who breathed our soul. The purpose of prayer is Christ.

9

LEAD ON, BRAVEHEART;
I WILL FOLLOW

"The true soldier fights not because he hates what is in front of him, but because he loves what is behind him."

—G. K. Chesterton

"One life is all we have and we live it as we believe in living it. But to sacrifice what you are and to live without belief, that is a fate more terrible than dying."

—St. Joan of Arc

I am sure most men have seen the movie *Braveheart*, the epic tale of Scottish independence. The main protagonist of the film is, of course, William Wallace, played by Mel Gibson. The other protagonist is Robert the Bruce, the man who became king of Scotland. In the film, he is a conflicted man who betrayed William Wallace only to come around and carry on his legacy. It seems as if the writers of the film took some poetic license in this area. In fact, Robert the Bruce was a loyal son of Scottish sovereignty from beginning to end. In truth, historians say that Robert the Bruce gave us the name Braveheart. William Wallace was a great hero, but the authors of the film blend the heroism of both men for the sake of the movie.

Before the tragedy of the Protestant Revolution, Scotland was a loyal son of the Church. Since then, different Scottish ethnic groups have remained faithful, but the glory of the Catholic Highlands has been lost for now. National sovereignty is a glorious tradition of Catholic civilization, and Robert the Bruce dreamt of an independent Scotland. It is hard for North American minds to understand, but Europe is a continent carved out by ethnic and family lines. The Scots trace their blood to the soil of the great patriarchs and clans that came before them. This is common among other European groups as well.

Patriotism is the virtue of honoring your father. The word *patriot* comes from the word *patria*, which pertains to fatherhood and refers to the fatherland. The next time someone asks if you support the patriarchy, emphatically reply, "Yes!" We are required to honor our father and mother, according to the Ten Commandments, which obliges us to patriotism. Robert the Bruce was not only a loyal son of the Scottish Highlands but also a loyal son of Rome. His great longing for an independent Scotland had come to fruition, but he still harbored great ambitions.

This was the era of the Crusades. The enemies of the Church have labeled the Crusades as a series of unjust religious wars, assuming that warring for religion is inherently unjust. Every war is a religious war because every war considers the value of the human person and the morality of taking lives. War by nature deals in eternity. Men join the military for a variety of reasons, but they fight for a very simple reason: men must fight an enemy. The expression that "there are no atheists in foxholes" is about more than the fear of death. Fearing death is half the equation; the other half is the fear of judgment. We do not fear death alone because we also fear the consequences of repaying what is owed according to how we have lived.

A man who stares death in the face ceases to be an atheist because death is unavoidably real. Atheism is a degenerate fantasy that dissolves when tested by the fires of hell. When the sun is shining and our bellies are full, we can ignore the Grim Reaper. We can convince ourselves that all we have is this life and that there is no afterlife. But when we face the prospect of heaven or hell, we let go of human philosophies. Death, judgment, heaven, and hell are four marks etched into the human heart. We cannot ignore them, and we must confront them. Soldiers who understand this are valiant and honorable but those who do not understand this become evil men. A man who believes not in eternal judgment becomes the judge of reality and justifies any action, moral or otherwise. Robert the Bruce was no such man.

Robert the Bruce desired to honor God even more than he desired to honor his nation. After a life of battle and service to his fatherland, he longed to go on a Crusade. For the heroes of Christendom, the Crusades were battles between Christ and the Antichrist. Saracen hordes had long pillaged and destroyed swaths of Christian civilization, and there was not a more glorious way to die than in battle for Our Lord. The men of this age did not hold to a fantasy of a "peaceful death," for they understood that the peace of Christ came with a sword (see Mt. 10:34). A life lived in comfort is fertile ground for the devil, especially when our twilight years are spent in avoidance of suffering. Christ will not be found without his cross, and we will not see salvation apart from a crucifixion.

As the king of Scotland approached the age of fifty-five, he suffered a stroke. As his death approached, he demanded a great promise from his close friend Sir James Douglas. Sir James vowed to take the physical heart of Robert the Bruce with him to the Holy Land. If the king could not take back the home of Christ from the Muhammadans with his bare hands, he would give his heart to be carried in the arms of his kin. Upon death, the heart of Robert the Bruce was cut out of his chest and prepared for the journey. Sir James Douglas carried the brave heart of King Robert in a silver casket. On the way to the Holy Land, Sir James stopped to help with the reconquest of Spain. Overwhelmed by a surprise attack, Sir James faced certain death. Before he marched toward his end, he took out the heart of Robert the Bruce. Holding up the heart of the king, he shouted to his men, "Lead on brave heart, now pass thou onward before us, as thou wast wont, and I will follow thee or die." He tossed the true Braveheart into the midst of his enemies and rushed toward Muhammad's militia. He died by the blade of a sword, cast down in service to the king.

How many of us would carry the heart of our king into battle? Sir James Douglas was a loyal servant to his king, but both men were first sons of the King of Kings. If Jesus Christ is to reign in heaven and on earth, then he must reign in your life. Even your own life must be expendable in the defense of the kingdom of Christ. The Lord is your general, you are his soldiers. Choose to die in battle, to follow the heart of the King. Heaven is full of heroes; hell is full of cowards. Enlist in the army of God or risk conscription in the draft of the demon.

The Crusade Is Overdue

"We fight not for glory, nor for wealth, nor honour but only and alone for freedom which no good man surrenders but with his life."

—Robert the Bruce

If you ask the average person about the Crusades, you will hear a variety of opinions, most of them negative. For some, the Crusades are a mythical era of Christian blood-lust against a peaceful Muhammadan civilization. They see the Crusaders as greedy conquerors who sought riches and power over a piece of land in the Middle East. Others do not have strong opinions on the matter but cannot understand how anyone would go to war over religion. These people have an idea that all religion is more or less a way to internal peace. They view religion as something that should be strictly personal. Those who believe the lies about the Crusaders and portray them as heinous villains are wrong about history. Those who believe religion should look more like mindfulness meditation than a battle for orthodoxy are wrong about religion.

There were dark moments in the Crusades to be sure, but this was the exception and not the rule. There were dark moments in World War II, but it is still celebrated for its triumph over Hitler. Furthermore, the Crusades were a series of battles spanning hundreds of years. When people appeal to the Crusades, they usually have no idea of even the century they have in mind, let alone the battle. St. John Henry Newman famously said, "To be deep in history is to cease to be Protestant." I would add that to navigate the depths of the Crusades is to desire to be a Crusader.

Many have a perception that Mohammedanism is an ancient religion that somehow grew out of the Middle East in an organic fashion. In truth, Mohammedanism is a heresy that violently emerged in Arabia six centuries after Christ. Muhammad was not a man of peace or a true prophet. He led armies against innocent people and forced conversions by the tip of the sword. He had multiple wives, loads of children that he did not raise, and was responsible for the deaths of thousands. He denied the divinity of Jesus Christ, the primacy of the Church, and the Canon of Scripture. His teachings allowed for soldiers to take sex slaves as the spoils of battle, and he married a six-year-old girl. Whatever your relationship may be with individual Mohammedans, of whom many are kind people, Muhammad was evil.

He thrust into the mind of fallen men a carnal religion that demanded nothing of self-control after the manner of Christianity. Mohammedan men are given free rein to have temporary wives—that is, mistresses—and non-Muslims are seen to be in the house of war. Saying these things in a public setting is dangerous in North America, which is evidence of the insanity of our society. Comedians and writers forge for themselves wealthy careers while espousing anti-Catholic dribble. Yet, criticizing Mohammedanism in public is a social mortal sin. It is said that if you stand for nothing, you will fall for anything. Our nations have ceased standing on the firmament of the Catholic Church, thus they have fallen into the abyss.

Christendom at the time of Muhammad spread through the majority of the territory carved out by the Roman

Empire. North and East Africa, Spain, the Holy Land, and the Middle East were fertile grounds of the Catholic faith. Within fifty years of the proliferation of the false prophet, two-thirds of the Christian world had been subjugated at the tip of the sword and by the promise of carnal pleasure. Millions of men had fallen prey to the unholy offer of virginal brides awaiting them in a false paradise. Millions of women mourned the loss of their martyred husbands as they now found themselves sex slaves of the mad militants of Mecca. The Catholic Church and her children had been attacked by a vicious antireligion, and history had been altered by one of its greatest tragedies. Whole populations recently freed from original sin were cast back into paganism by maniacs who denied the Holy Trinity. Christendom had taken a mortal blow. Spain was lost, and Mohammedan hoards made their way within a stone's throw of Paris. Not since Hannibal came thundering over the Italian Alps with African elephants had Rome seen such a demon let loose from the North African desert.

After three centuries of bloodshed and an exponential damnation of souls, Pope Urban II set the stage for the onset of the First Crusade. Throughout Europe, there had been regional success and resistance to the Saracen slaughter, but Europe had reached a breaking point. Never before had Christ's Church seen such an onslaught. Barbarian tribes and warlords had breached Christendom before, but never with a hatred and rejection of Christ as their battle cry. At stake was not only regional power but a dichotomy of dominion. Men of all ages and from all bloodlines would have to choose: king or sultan.

Deus Vult!

"It is not the victory that makes the joy of noble hearts, but the combat."

—Count Charles Forbes René de Montalembert

No earthly force would do, no amount of arrows could abrogate the spiritual nemesis whirling out of the Arabian deserts. The ancestral home of Adam, Abraham, and Noah had been usurped. What was needed was not a war but an *exorcism*. The Crusaders were called to cast the devil's heretical prophets into the abyss and out of Jerusalem, as St. Michael had done to the dragon. The authority of generals and kings could only go so far. It was the authority of God himself, through the commander of the *Mysticum Corpus Christi* who rallied the soldiers of salvation. Pope Urban II bellowed forth a call to arms rivaling that of St. Peter at Pentecost. According to chronicler Robert the Monk, at the Council of Clermont, the pope delivered the following message:

> Oh race of Franks, race from across the mountains, race beloved and chosen by God—as is clear from many of your works—set apart from all other nations by the situation of your country as well as by your Catholic faith and the honor which you render to the holy Church: to you our discourse is addressed, and for you our exhortations are intended. We wish you to know what a grievous cause has led us to your country, for it is the imminent peril threatening you and all the faithful which has brought us hither.
>
> From the confines of Jerusalem and from the city of Constantinople a grievous report has gone forth and has repeatedly been brought to our ears; namely, that a race from the kingdom of the Persians, an accursed race, a race

wholly alienated from God, *a generation that set not their heart aright and whose spirit was not steadfast with God* (Ps. lxxvii. 8), violently invaded the lands of those Christians and has depopulated them by pillage and fire. They have led away a part of the captives into their own country, and a part they have killed by cruel tortures. They have either destroyed the churches of God or appropriated them for the rites of their own religion. They destroy the altars, after having defiled them with their uncleanness. . . . The kingdom of the Greeks is now dismembered by them and has been deprived of territory so vast in extent that it could be traversed in two months' time.

On whom, therefore, is the labor of avenging these wrongs and of recovering this territory incumbent, if not upon you, you upon whom, above all other nations, God has conferred remarkable glory in arms, great courage, bodily activity, and strength to humble the heads of those who resist you? Let the deeds of your ancestors encourage you and incite your minds to manly achievements: the greatness of King Charlemagne, and of his son Louis, and of your other monarchs, who have destroyed the kingdoms of the Turks and have extended the sway of the Church over lands previously possessed by the pagan. Let the holy sepulcher of our Lord and Saviour, which is possessed by unclean nations, especially arouse you, and the holy places which are now treated, with ignominy and irreverently polluted with the filth of the unclean. Oh, most valiant soldiers and descendants of invincible ancestors, do not degenerate our progenitors, but recall the valor of your progenitors.

But if you are hindered by love of children, parents, or of wife, remember what the Lord says in the Gospel, *He that loveth father or mother more than me is not worthy of me* (Mt. x. 37), *every one that hath forsaken houses, or brethren, or sisters, or father, or mother, or wife, or children, or lands, for my name's sake, shall receive an hundredfold, and shall inherit everlasting life* (Mt. xix. 29). Let none of your possessions retain you, nor solicitude for your family affairs. For this land which you inhabit, shut in on all sides by the seas and surrounded by the mountain peaks, is too narrow for your large population; nor does it abound in wealth; and it furnishes scarcely food enough for its cultivators. Hence it is that you murder and devour one another, that you wage war, and that very many among you perish in intestinal strife.

Let hatred therefore depart from among you, let your quarrels end, let wars cease, and let all dissensions and controversies slumber. Enter upon the road to the Holy Sepulcher, wrest that land from the wicked race, and subject it to yourselves. That land which, as the Scripture says, *floweth with milk and honey* (cf. Dt. xxvi. 9) was given by God into the power of the children of Israel. Jerusalem is the center of the earth; the land is fruitful above all others, like another paradise of delights. The Redeemer of mankind had made this spot illustrious by His advent, has beautified it by His sojourn, has consecrated it by His passion, has redeemed it by His death, has glorified it by His burial.

This royal city, however, situated at the center of the earth, is now held captive by the enemies of Christ and is subjected, by those who do not know God, to the worship of the heathen. She seeks, therefore, and desires to be liberated and ceases not to implore you to come to her aid. From you especially she asks succour, because as we have already said, God has conferred upon you above all other nations great glory in arms. Accordingly, undertake this journey eagerly for the remission of your sins, with the assurance of the reward of imperishable glory in the kingdom of heaven.

The chronicler then states:

When Pope Urban had urbanely said these and very similar things, he so centered in one purpose the desires all who were present that all cried out, God wills it! God wills it! [*Deus vult! Deus vult!*] When the venerable Roman pontiff heard that, with eyes uplifted to heaven, he gave thanks to God and, commanding silence with his hand, said:

Most beloved brethren, today is manifest in you what the Lord says in the Gospel, *Where two or three are gathered together in my name, there am I in the midst of them* (Mt.

xviii. 20) for unless God had been present in your spirits, all of you would not have uttered the same cry; since, although the cry issued from numerous mouths, yet the origin of the cry as one. Therefore I say to you that God, who is implanted in your breasts, has drawn it forth from you. Let that be your war cry in combats, because it is given to you by God. When an armed attack is made upon the enemy, this one cry be raised by all the soldiers of God: '*Deus vult! Deus vult!*'

Whoever, therefore, shall determine upon this holy pilgrimage, and shall make his vow to God to that effect, and shall offer himself to Him for sacrifice, as a living victim, holy and acceptable to God, shall wear the sign of the cross of the Lord on his forehead or on his breast. When, indeed, he shall return from his journey, having fulfilled his vow, let him place the cross on his back between his shoulders. Thus shall ye, indeed, by this twofold action, fulfill the precept of the Lord, as in the Gospel, *he that taketh not his cross, and followeth after me, is not worthy of me* (Mt. x. 38).

Catholicism is a manly religion; it is a *fighting religion*. Every member of the Body of Christ is called from the devil's camp at baptism (one of the meanings of the word s*acrament* is "military oath"). We are promoted at confirmation and receive fighting strength in the Eucharist. Orders are commanded to us by the priest in the confessional that we are to *go and sin no more*. Let no one fool you—we are not pacifists. We are called to holy violence (see Mt. 11:12). Like Christ who cleanses the Temple, showing us the power of the Rosary in his knotted scourge, we too are called. The Crusades of the past may be over, but the call to defend the Church and her patrimony still stands.

There is perhaps no greater example of masculine virtue in the history of Catholicism than the example of the Crusaders: They followed the call of a holy pope, and risked their lives for the will of God. They carried their Crosses in the form of a sword, and they gave their bleeding hearts for the glory of Christendom. We are not worthy to call these men ancestors, but we can repay them by following their example.

Each day when we rise, the call of *Deus Vult* should be on our mind. God's will is the warrior's plan and the mold that fashions heroes. The enemies of Christ have not stopped their onslaught, and they come in an array of forms. Heathenry still seeks to pull souls back to Satan. Politicians work to degrade the moral framework of our civilization. Pornographers aim at the innocence of children, and sexual deviants aspire to enlist the youth in their legions.

The armies of the devil have changed their tactics, seldom seeking the death of the Christian. Satan has lost too many souls to martyrdom and instead conscripts souls into his cult by way of comfort. Our popes may not be calling fighting men to battle, but Our Lord still beckons us to join the heavenly host. St. Michael still commands his post as the general of heaven's special forces, and he longs for a return to war.

Answer the call of your fathers who pray for you tirelessly in the temple of the heavenly Jerusalem. They gave their lives and worldly possessions so they could offer themselves as a living sacrifice for their progeny. Most died deaths unrecorded by history, and only a few made it home. They stormed the captured cities and lost life and limb to set the captives free. Like Christ, they *descended into the dead*, and like Christ, when the spear pierced their hearts, they beheld the face of God. We know not their names, but their blood runs through our veins. Men of Europe call them *grandfather*, Christian men of other nations call them *liberator*.

How long must we watch the serpent slither in and out of our homes? How long can we stand under the weight of heresy in our Church? At what point do we say enough is enough?

The responsibility is on our shoulders to rebuild Christendom. The Crusaders showed us the way, and they wait from beyond the grave for us to pick up our swords. It is this point in history that our children's children will read of in years to come. When they look to their ancestors, they will look honorably or shamefully at the actions of their forefathers. Are we to leave a legacy worthy of a Crusader, or will we fade into history, not worthy of a mention? Decide.

10

HEAR ME AND UNDERSTAND WELL, MY LITTLE SON

"If anyone does not wish to have Mary Immaculate for his Mother, he will not have Christ for his Brother."

—St. Maximillian Kolbe

"You never go away from us, yet we have difficulty in returning to You. Come, Lord, stir us up and call us back. Kindle and seize us. Be our fire and our sweetness. Let us love. Let us run."

—St. Augustine of Hippo

FOR years, I lived in mortal sin. I need not explain which sins or the extent thereof; however, I was not living as a man dedicated to Our Lord and Our Lady. As a child and adolescent, I did have a semblance of faith in Jesus Christ. Young children easily take to the reality of God because they are not darkened by sin and inane philosophy. I was no different. There was a period of time when I prayed consistently, and for a while, I attended Mass as a teenager. I knew God was real in a tangible way, but I had no protection against the wickedness and snares of the devil. I rarely received the sacraments and never had a meaningful confession until adulthood.

As most men do, I fell for the traps of the world, the flesh, and the devil. By the time my undergraduate degree was complete, I had given in to the trickery of atheist-inspired reasoning. I studied French, Spanish, and Italian, and in most cases, we read so-called Enlightenment era literature. This meant our reading was in most cases anti-Catholic, although at times a glimmer of Christ snuck through. I was a prideful man, puffed up by my ego and self-reliance. I believed in my autonomy as the master of my own soul. I believed I could carve my destiny in any manner I saw fit.

It is a common lie told to young people today that they can *be anything they want*. Like most demonic deceptions, this is partly true. To a degree, we can forge a path for ourselves by our own efforts and free will. We can make choices and pursue our interests; many who do this live relatively successful lives. Nevertheless, we are not the Creator, we are the creatures. In our quest for individual autonomy and destiny, we so often seek after the forbidden fruit. We seek the knowledge of things that are only proper to God, and in doing so, we seek *to become like gods*.

I was guilty of many sins and, like the man presented in chapter 4, I had fallen into modern paganism. I worshiped the human sciences; I worshiped the cult of politics; I worshiped the gods of progress and the human body. I believed that man was *evolving*, moving toward better things with each passing moment. I believed that we could control the forces of nature and the reality of truth. I did not know it at the time, but I believed the same things that made Lucifer fall. I served myself and my beliefs and was shaping my life in order to say *"my will be done."*

Through God's creativity, he somehow cast down my pride and self-worship. In ways unbeknownst to me, I was provided with particular graces that led me to a reconsideration of the Catholic faith. The demon still had free rein in my intellect, as I was not living in a state of grace, but my guardian angel must have been fighting ferociously. One day, I will find out who was praying for me, but it must have been someone holy. I was so far gone intellectually that it is a miracle I reconsidered Catholicism.

But then I found employment in a Catholic school board, and I found myself surrounded by Catholics and Catholicism.

More than anything, I hated hypocrisy, thus I was not going to teach in a system that professed a faith I did not believe. If I was going to teach in Catholic schools, I was going to be Catholic. In the lead up to Teachers College, I started to reconsider certain questions about God. While at Teachers College, I read and studied to the point that I was comfortable with professing the Faith, albeit a watered-down liberalized version. In that first year as a Catholic school teacher, God and his angels kept up an unrelenting onslaught of grace against my feeble defenses.

God's grace flows like water proceeding from a waterfall. When we sin, we build dams to guard ourselves from him, and it is possible for us to permanently block the stream of divine grace. My dam was strong, but by this grace, so was my curiosity. I heard the sound of whitewater smashing against my defenses, and I was tired of fortifying a structure that cut me off from my Maker. As proud as I was, I still followed my ideas through to their logical conclusion. Because of this, I came to understand that on my side of

the dam was a life of illusion and despair. I decided not
to follow the culture's program of depression, evil images,
broken families, Luciferian liberalism and self-medication.
I had seen the tempter's tricks and breathed the dragon's
breath. I was not going to build a family rooted in the per-
verted logic of a decaying civilization. I knew that the past
was full of heroes and that I was not one of them. It was
clear that something fully alive and free lay beyond the
wall. The raging river of redemption roared too loud to be
ignored. For so long, I had drunk the devil's draught to the
dregs and I needed a Savior. But first, I needed the woman
who specializes in snake stomping. I needed the queen to
bring me home to the King of Kings.

The Woman Who Saved My Soul

*"Am I not here, who is your Mother? Are you not under my pro-
tection? Am I not your health? Are you not happily within my
fold? What else do you wish? Do not grieve nor be disturbed by
anything."*

—Our Lady of Guadalupe

Man has to live with the consequences of the Fall. Like
Adam, we work among the thorns and thistles, eating by
the sweat of our brow, only to return to dust. Without God,
life is unbearable. It is no wonder that a society replete with
atheist materialism is becoming more and more suicidal.
Referendums about destroying unborn children are held in
formerly Catholic countries, where people celebrate this
legalization. Murdering the elderly is marketed as dying
with dignity, as if being put down like a dog is in keeping

with the dignity of those made in the image and likeness of God. Young people consecrate themselves to Satan by swearing oaths against having children to save the climate. And male and female bodies are seen as interchangeable outfits that can be acquired through hormones and surgery. Never has it been clearer that we live and work among the thorns. Since the universal flood of Noah, this may be the most depraved time in history.

But through the thorns come roses. Through the briars of barbarism, God sends people into your life in the most unexpected ways. Sometimes they come in the form of angels; sometimes they come in the form of friends. Somehow, through a series of forgettable work functions, I became friends with someone who believed in and listened to God. This was new for me. I had been around so-called Catholics all my life but never around people who sought to live a life of prayer. A person seeking holiness and union with Christ was a novelty.

This newfound friend of mine took a risk and invited me to chaperone a mission to Mexico City. I studied Spanish for years and had dreamt of teaching the language to high school students. Instead, I found myself teaching French to elementary school students in a school board that did not offer Spanish. God knows best, and I now see that all those years of language study prepared me for the mission that became my life's mission. This friend and I had spoken only a few times, yet she listened to the promptings of the Holy Ghost and brought me to Mexico.

The week spent in Mexico City stands as a timeless moment in my memory. The mission setting was in a garbage dump, serving the poorest of the poor. This was a true Catholic mission, not a glorified social justice trip. We served the physical and spiritual needs of the inhabitants of the shanty homes, and through them, we encountered the Lord Jesus. I have never been to war, but I imagine the radical interior transformation that soldiers go through is something like what I experienced. I saw death and disease, neglect and despair. Yet, amid the filth of Mexico City's refuse, I saw God.

We began the week with a pilgrimage to Our Lady of Guadalupe, the site of the Marian apparition that brought the Americas to the Faith. I am embarrassed to say that I had no idea who Our Lady of Guadalupe was. Of course, I knew who Mary was, but I knew nothing of apparitions. Furthermore, the thought of the Queen of Heaven and Earth appearing to speak with human beings seemed like fantasy. This was our first of two visits to the shrine of Our Lady, and although I saw the historical significance and beauty of the location, I missed the point.

At the end of our week, we had another pilgrimage sched-uled. The day before we returned to visit Our Lady, we had Holy Mass in the garbage dump. We erected a tarp overhead and used a folding table as the altar. There were no pews, and the setting was a far cry from a Gothic cathedral. I am as traditionalist as you can be; I love Latin, incense, chant, and beautiful vestments. However, the raw nature and simplicity of this setting made manifest that we were on a mission to bring Christ to lost souls. Yet, it was not the inhabitants of the dump who were lost; it was me. I was a lost soul and had to travel across a continent to find my home.

Then something happened. After Holy Communion, I dropped to my knees in the dust. I laid my head in my hands and wept. To dust Adam returns, and at the tomb of the dead man, Jesus weeps. I was Adam, expelled from the garden, dead in my sin. For the first time in my life, I knew that I wasn't anything other than a sinner. My education, my achievements, my worldly pleasures—nothing could keep me from kneeling. I was never a depressed man, but I saw my life as the valley of tears it truly was.

On the final day of our mission, we again visited the shrine of Our Lady of Guadalupe. For those who have never been there, the shrine is at the top of a hill. It takes a few minutes to walk up, and with the elevation of Mexico City, it is not an easy task. On this day, I was as determined as I have ever been at any moment in my life. I awoke with a strong headache and did not have much of an appetite. Nevertheless, I raced up the hill with reckless abandon. Something in my soul knew that I was sick, and I needed to see my Mother. The whole group visited the shrine to start the visit, and we had the option to stay at the shrine or explore the grounds. Without hesitation, I stayed in the shrine.

In my pocket, I had a plastic rosary. I had never prayed with it; however, I carried it with me since I received it a year and a half earlier. I do not know if I ever prayed a full Rosary in my life before this moment. Still, I knelt before the altar dedicated to our Mother and began to pray the Rosary. I know now that I prayed incorrectly. I prayed the Our Father on the crucifix, the Glory Be on the Our Father beads, and the Hail Mary on the proper beads. Even so, I prayed this improper Rosary twice. I am not a small man, but the time spent kneeling on the hard marble floor was painless. After I had prayed with the rosary, I sat in a chair roughly twenty feet from the altar. For almost two hours, I sat there in silence, my head down, listening to the Virgin.

The shrine is located where Our Lady appeared to St. Juan Diego. He expressed to the Virgin in one of their encounters that he was worried about his sick uncle. Our Blessed Mother said in response:

> Hear me and understand well, my little son, that nothing should frighten or grieve you. Let not your heart be disturbed. Do not fear that sickness, nor any other sickness or anguish. Am I not here, who is your Mother? Are you not under my protection? Am I not your health? Are you not happily within my fold? What else do you wish? Do not grieve nor be disturbed by anything. Do not be afflicted by the illness of your uncle, who will not die now from it. Be assured that he is now cured. Climb, my dear son, to the top of the hill.

Throughout this time with Our Lady, it was as if she said the same thing to me. I feared the sickness in my soul; my heart was tired and I wretched with anguish over my sins. In an instant, I knew that Mary was my health, my protection, and that I would not lose my soul just yet. By some immeasurable undeserved grace, I had been spared from damnation. So often I had lived as if there was no God, as if I was the maker of my destiny. But now, I knew I was her son and that I had to climb out of the pit and up to God.

For years, I justified to myself all that I had done. But without argument, Mary made very clear to me all my faults. I sat there, weeping and nodding my head at each interior revelation. A slide show of my life played before my eyes, and I knew the weight of my transgressions. She held out her hand and walked me toward the cross. From the foot of the Crucifixion, I stared up at Our Lord. I saw the blood that flowed from his crown of thorns wedged into his flesh by my sinfulness. I heard the heaviness of his breath as he begged God to forgive my ignorance. I saw my handprints on the hammer that drove in the nails.

Heavyweight boxing champion Mike Tyson famously said, "*Everyone has a plan until they get punched in the mouth.*" I would add that every man plans to justify his sin until he stands in front of his Mother. The shame of offending the Most Holy Virgin was more painful than anything I had experienced. No amount of rationalization or argument remained. My Mother knew best.

Only one week before the mission, my wife and I found out she was pregnant with our first child. At the time, I did not know that Our Lady of Guadalupe is the patroness of the unborn. But in that time spent with her, I fell in love with the son I had never met and was convicted of the weight of my impending fatherhood. Upon my return to Canada, I knew that my life had to change. My marriage had to change, my habits had to change, and the direction of my life had to change. My wife and I worked through this newfound faith, and although it was difficult in the beginning, our marriage finally became God-centered. I was a man of the world when I arrived in Mexico, and I was *a son of Rome* when I returned home.

The Holy Virgin of Guadalupe saved my soul. She brought me home to God. I owe the Blessed Mother my whole being without reserve. I am still a wretched sinner and rely daily on the power of the Rosary. But I am a mama's boy, and I will call her blessed all the days of my life.

OUR ONLY HOPE

"Give me an army saying the Rosary and I will conquer the world."

—Blessed Pope Pius IX

"There is no problem, I tell you, no matter how difficult it is, that we cannot solve by the prayer of the Holy Rosary."

—Sister Lucia of Fatima

THE tradition of praying the Hail Mary begins in the New Testament when the Angel Gabriel says "Hail, full of grace, the Lord is with thee: blessed art thou among women" (Lk. 1:28). Upon Mary's visit to her cousin Elizabeth, the mother of St. John the Baptist, she is filled with the Holy Ghost and exclaims, "Blessed is the fruit of thy womb" (Lk. 1:42). For centuries, Catholics recited these Scripture passages as part of what became the Ave Maria that we know today. It is not clear when exactly the second half of the prayer became the norm. But intercessory prayer is as ancient as the Church, and we know that Mary prayed at the foot of the cross at the hour of Our Lord's death. Thus, asking the Blessed Mother to "pray for us sinners now and at the hour of our death" is only fitting.

Protestants often reject the Blessed Mother, which is unbiblical, as Mary clearly states in the Gospel of St. Luke, "Because he hath regarded the humility of his handmaid; for behold from henceforth all generations shall call me blessed" (Lk. 1:48). The Sacred Scriptures, inspired by the Holy Ghost, tell us that *all generations* will call the Mary blessed. One reason why this prerogative is dictated to us by God through St. Luke's Gospel is to remind us of the incarnational element of our Faith. God, in his infinite wisdom, chose a woman to bring forth the Savior. The heavenly Father desires that even the physical aspect of his creation be redeemed.

Throughout history, we see a variety of heresies and demonically inspired movements opposed to the Church. Without fail, these heretical movements always fall into the errors of Gnosticism, Materialism, or Arianism. In the twelfth and thirteenth centuries, a diabolical heresy known as Albigensianism spread like a plague throughout the eldest daughter of the Church, France. French Catholics were swept away with a dualist movement that encouraged people to commit suicide and even starve their children to death. Albigensianism promoted belief in an evil god, who was the god of material things, and a good god, who was the god of spiritual things. Matter was evil and the spirit was good. They believed in the transmigration of souls, meaning that souls could exist in different bodies. Furthermore, procreation was condemned, as was marriage, because it placed value on new human life. According to this hellish insanity, Jesus Christ had no body, was not considered true God, and Mary was certainly not his mother. Doubtless, this was an arch-heresy, a dangerous religious belief that sought to confirm souls in mortal sin and damnation. It was a synthesis of previous errors, Gnostic and Arian, and represented the worst of all worlds.

According to pious tradition, Our Lady appeared to St. Dominic who at that time faced this heresy head on. St. Dominic was instructed by Our Lady to *preach her psalter*. This referred to what was then considered the Marian psalter, which meant a tradition of praying 150 *Aves*. This corresponded to the 150 psalms chanted every week by the monks and priests. This directive from Our Lady is so unique because she instructed St. Dominic to preach the Rosary along with the traditional fifteen mysteries. Each mystery carried with it a meditation that refuted the Albigensian heresy. In each mystery of the Rosary, our attention is placed on bodily and physical acts of Our Lord and Our Lady. From the Annunciation to the Crucifixion to the Coronation of Mary in heaven, we contemplate God's interaction with the realm of created things.

Not only was St. Dominic's preaching of the Rosary wrought with miracles and success, but devotion to the Rosary even inspired great military success. St. Louis de Montfort recounts that Count Simon de Montfort won a major battle against the Albigensians under the patronage of Our Lady of the Rosary. The Crusaders were outnumbered by tens of thousands and experienced virtually no casualties.

Centuries later, the Rosary was again the backbone of a definitive battle against that old enemy, the Mohammedans. Pope St. Pius V urged all of Europe to pray the Rosary to help Catholic naval fleets in an otherwise impossible battle against the Ottoman Turks. Against great odds, the

Christians defeated the Mohammedan armies at the Gulf of Patras. It is said that the sea was made purple with blood due to the tens of thousands of casualties. Pope St. Pius V was mystically shown that the Catholics had won in a vision at the moment of victory. He then instituted the feast day of Our Lady of Victory, celebrated October 7th. Many other such victories have been won over the centuries.

Brazil in 1964 was on the brink of a Communist take-over. As a defense, the archbishop of Rio de Janeiro implored the people of Brazil to live out the message of Fatima and rely on the Rosary against Communism. The president of the nation was so upset that he publicly ridiculed the Rosary. Take a moment and think how motivated you would be if someone publicly insulted your mother. That same righteous anger and hatred of the devil gave a divine spark to the people of Brazil. Within days of these events, twenty thousand women prayed the Rosary in the midst of a Communist rally. The sound of their prayers was so deafening that the organizers had to stop the event. It was as if their voices were amplified in union with the choirs of angels. Shortly after, six hundred thousand citizens marched through Rio de Janeiro praying to Our Lady. The Communists were horrified. Heaven had opened a portal to release holy wrath upon them. Within two weeks, the Communists were ousted from the country, and the very next day, over one million people marched in a prayer of thanksgiving, once again relying on the beads of the holy scourge of the Rosary.

Our culture faces another Albigensian heresy. Hoards of people believe in the same gnostic tenants of that diabolical deception. Like the heretics of the thirteenth century, the body is seen as an expendable object with which we may do what we will. Suicide is promoted as a way to be free from suffering. There is no freedom without suffering, because there is no Christ without the cross. Climate alarmists spend millions promoting a childless life as to not burden the earth. Children are abused by the fallacious ideology that they can mutilate their bodies in order to match how they feel inside. The fallen angel of the Albigensians has returned in disguise. Our civilization continues to fight the invasion of a visceral hatred of the Faith by those who wish its destruction. Open Communism and Socialism are discussed in classrooms as a method to revolt against the ancient order of Christendom.

The only hope we have is the Most Holy Rosary of the Virgin Mary. The only true weapon is the scourge of the psalter of the Blessed Virgin. Men have sat back as effeminate bystanders for too long. In the absence of leaders and heroes, the legions of doom have run rampant throughout our families and society. Our Church is suffering due to the lack of men in the pews and the lack of men on their knees. St. Paul warns us of these times: "For there shall be a time, when they will not endure sound doctrine; but, according to their own desires, they will heap to themselves teachers, having itching ears: And will indeed turn away their hearing from the truth, but will be turned unto fables. But be thou vigilant, labour in all things, do the work of an evangelist, fulfill thy ministry. Be sober" (2 Tim. 4:3–5).

These are the days when men chase after scientism and fantasy as if it were gospel truth. These are the days when men turn away from hearing the truth because their spines are too slouched to stand up to criticism. It is required that we answer the call to repent for the sin of Adam and unite ourselves to the cross of Christ. We must *rejoice* in our suffering and seek to "fill up those things that are wanting of the sufferings of Christ" (Col. 1:24). Only a holy life filled with holy sacrifice and a holy death will please God as a living sacrifice in these times. "For what doth it profit a man, if he gain the whole world, and suffer the loss of his own soul?" (Mt. 16:26).

What is stopping you from being the man Christ calls you to be? Do the demons of adultery still call forth from the satanic playground of addiction to evil images? Does the bottle still bellow for you to drink to your own demise? Have you still the rage of an unhinged man when business matters fall through? Do you sacrifice time with your family in order to appease the gods of prosperity?

Remember, Jesus Christ says: "If thy eye scandalize thee, pluck it out. It is better for thee with one eye to enter into the kingdom of God, than having two eyes to be cast into the hell of fire: Where their worm dieth not, and the fire is not extinguished" (Mk. 9:46–47).

If you have been inspired by anything in this book, it is time to make the necessary changes. All things that tether you to a disordered attachment to the world, the flesh, or the devil need to be cast into the fire. Break off the chains of sin and vice so that you can be free to ascend with Christ on the last day.

Be the man your wife dreamt of as a child. G. K. Chesterton reminds us that children love fairy tales not because they want to hear of dragons, for they know dragons are real; they love fairy tales because they want to see how *dragons are defeated*. No matter your age or state in life, you are called to be a dragon slayer. Our women and children so often wait in prisons guarded by fire-breathing demons. Our addictions, our slothfulness, our selfishness, and our effeminacy all supply endless amounts of fuel to the flames.

Just as Christ carried the weight of our sin on his mighty shoulders, so too must we carry our loved ones up the mountain to the cross. Our Lord died so that the Queen of Heaven and her children may live. The only way to defeat the dragon is through unyielding courage in the face of death. A true knight, a true warrior, is the man who suffers the consequence of iniquity and overcomes. We are not here to be happy in the way that the world tells us to; true happiness is found in a life of holiness. We are not here to live lives of comfort; we are here to comfort the afflicted by sharing in their pain.

Depend on the Blessed Mother, for she waits at the foot of the cross for you to hang beside Our Lord. She rests on bended knee, veiled with the wedding veil of the Eternal Spouse of the Holy Ghost. Wed your sufferings to the seven sorrows of her heart. Lay down your pride and self-love and look into your Mother's eyes. It is the Virgin who weeps for you when you fall. It is the Queen of the Angels who takes your hand and brings you to your Father. The Most Holy Mother of the Messiah will never stop loving her sons.

She knows you are tired; she knows you are weary. She knows your burden is too heavy to carry alone. Therefore, listen to her Son: "Come to me, all you that labour, and are burdened, and I will refresh you. Take up my yoke upon you, and learn of me, because I am meek, and humble of heart: and you shall find rest to your souls. For my yoke is sweet and my burden light" (Mt. 11:28–30).

Be not the man who picked up this book; instead, be the man who lives by this book. Be not the man you were when Christ first called you; instead, be the man who Christ died for you to be. Do not disappoint your Mother; instead, please her by following the will of your Father. The hour has come to be more than just a man. The hour has come to be a *man of God, a Terror of Demons.*

Deus vult!

EPILOGUE

LITANY OF ST. JOSEPH, TERROR OF DEMONS

The following series of articles is used with the permission of the Fatima Center. I originally wrote this series over the winter of 2019–2020 as a spiritual exercise to help myself and others grow in devotion to St. Joseph. I have selected certain names from the Litany of St. Joseph and expanded on their meaning, using both theological traditions and my own literary imagination. I hope that the reader will see St. Joseph come alive throughout these pages and be inspired to devote himself to the Terror of Demons, St. Joseph.

BEFORE we talk about St. Joseph, I want to go back to some of the aspects of man's creation. We will use this to then talk about St. Joseph. As I have discussed in this book, the Church—and as a result, our society—is suffering from a plague of effeminacy, or softness. As I said, the Latin word *vir* is the word for man and is also the word for hero, husband, and person of courage, honor, and nobility. *Vir* is related to *virtus*, or virtue, but it is also used for excellence, bravery, courage, power, worth, manliness, and character. In the Latin Vulgate, Eve is called the *virago*, which means "heroic maiden" and "acts in a manly way."

When Adam calls Eve *virago*, it is not only a title of honor given to his wife but also a prefiguration of the

147

Virgin Mary, who is the fulfillment of what it means to be a true heroic maiden. It is interesting that in the first chapter of Genesis, the word *homo* (*hominem*) is used by God to classify the creation of man: *Et creavit Deus hominem ad imaginem suam* (And God created man to his own image, Gen. 1:27). *Homo* is the general word used most often for mankind or human being and is used here rather than the word *vir*, which pertains specifically to men. If you search the entire Latin Vulgate, you will only find the word *virago* used once. This surely has various implications, but one thing is sure: it is presupposed that man is to be a *vir*. Since the word *virago* means "acting in a manly way," it is reasonable to assume that the nature of *vir* is already known. Implicit in man's design by God is to be virtuous, manly, heroic, courageous, excellent, and strong. Man is the model for woman, and she finds her strength and resolve in his virtue. On average, men today act nothing like the *vir* they were made to be.

Contained in this reality is the biblical wisdom of the headship of man in his home and the submission of woman to her husband. Once again, our world may reject this, as it has been infected by the festering disease of feminism, but it is nonetheless the right order by which God himself ordained things. The root meaning of the word *submit* is to be "under the mission of" someone. Adam was created as the *vir* to lead the *virago* on a heroic mission of virtue and excellence, and Eve was created with the privilege of assisting in this endeavor. We've already discussed how this story goes. Almost immediately after the creation, Adam failed in his duty while allowing Eve to dialogue with the devil. God's proper order was not rectified until the New Eve said *fiat* and the New Adam exhibited the commensurate self-sacrifice necessary to undo the Fall.

I am sure that many have contemplated Our Lord's role as the New Adam, the crucified *Vir*. In addition, Mary is rightly called and venerated as the New Eve. She perfectly fulfills the title of *virago* and also Mother of the Living, as through her we access her Son, who gives eternal life. There is, however, a third key person who helps undo the snare of the ancient serpent. This man deserves greater devotion and contemplation: his name is Joseph.

Jesus and Mary sanctify and correct the errors of Adam and Eve in obvious ways: Jesus atones for the original sin, and Mary is the prophesied woman who crushes the serpent. However, an aspect of Adam and Eve's primordial relationship that cannot be overlooked is their spousal union. Mary is espoused to the Holy Ghost in a mystical sense, and Christ is espoused in an analogous way to his bride, the Church. But God also ordained the earthly marriage of Mary and Joseph to show us a perfect model of what Adam and Eve failed to fulfill in their time.

Mary and Joseph's marriage was not symbolic or for external pretense. It is a teaching of the Faith that their marriage was a true marriage. Moreover, it was not only theological or mystical but also lived in space and time. It is an incarnational way for the bond of husband and wife to be made holy once again. Where Adam and Eve fail in fidelity to God's commands, Joseph and Mary thrive in prayerful obedience. Where Adam and Eve give in to the appetites of the flesh and partake in the forbidden fruit, Joseph and

Mary live in perfect continence, demonstrating the perfect chastity based in an unyielding love of God.[1]

Jesus is the new Adam and Mary is the new Eve, but after them, glorious St. Joseph is rightly given *protodulia*, meaning that among the saints, he is given first place.[2] Put simply, in a similar way to Mary being "the woman," Joseph is "the man."

We need Joseph in these times. We need the man who raised Our Lord to teach us to be men. We need the man who cared for the Mother of God to teach us how to treat the mother of our children. All men, whether they are biological fathers or spiritual fathers, must look to St. Joseph as their guide.

St. Joseph, Lover of Poverty

To be an upright Catholic man in today's "modernity" is an exercise in being counter-cultural and waging an unremitting counterrevolution, striving to restore God's right order

---

1   It is a common interpretation among Church Fathers that Eve committed a sin of lust by giving in to a physical appetite that was mortally sinful. Of course, Adam partook in this sin as well.

2   *Latria* is the theological term for the worship of God alone. This worship can only be given to God. *Dulia* is the word for veneration given to saints, which is of a much lesser degree but still an act of honor. It is helpful to use these terms because in English both can be rendered "worship," especially in many older Catholic prayers and literary works. *Hyperdulia*, the greatest of *dulia*, is then the proper term for the unique veneration we give our Blessed Mother. *Protodulia* is then the "first place *dulia*" after the highest *dulia* (*hyperdulia*), which is the singular veneration we render unto St. Joseph.

at every level of society. We must reject the trappings of the world in order to live a virtuous life.

To love poverty does not only entail financial austerity. It is possible to be financially poor but have no concept of poverty, and conversely, it is possible to be wealthy and to understand the meaning of poverty. Poverty itself has no intrinsic goodness, and in many cases, it is a burden. However, the practice of poverty is a practice in virtue. The benefit of practicing poverty is found in self-denial and cultivation of the cardinal virtues. Great fortitude and temperance is required to adopt poverty in one's life. Furthermore, prudence is required to discern between necessary and unnecessary things, and almsgiving enables one to live a life of greater justice.

St. Joseph demonstrated his love for poverty in the Gospels; however, I would argue that his greatest acceptance of poverty is largely missed. To be sure, St. Joseph embraced an austere life as a craftsman and humble father. The birth of Christ in a cave, the Flight to Egypt, and his laborious occupation all demonstrate his detachment from worldly goods. However, his chastity, in my opinion, is his greatest demonstration of true poverty. Poverty does not only mean eschewing material things, but it is ultimately about sacrifice. We embrace poverty when we willingly deny ourselves the greatest of pleasures and comforts. Sacrifice is supposed to hurt, and it is ordained toward a greater good.

Joseph embraced the call to holy purity in his unique marriage to the Blessed Mother. In doing so, he demonstrated a great sacrifice and love of poverty. He loved the Mother of God more than any of us can ever understand, yet he guarded her virginity and kept her inviolate. The children at Fatima described the Virgin Mary as the most beautiful woman imaginable. Some theologians and artists depict Joseph as an older man in an attempt to make his great chastity seem more feasible. But there is great reason to believe that he was a young, strong, and virile man, which in fact makes his chastity that much more heroic.[3] St. Francis de Sales, Cornelius a Lapide, Francisco Suarez, and St. Alphonsus Ligouri all teach that St. Joseph was sanctified and regenerated in his mother's womb prior to birth. He had perfect control of his passions and temperaments; thus, he was able to admire the beauty of Mary, yet still practice perfect continence.

None of us have been sanctified in our mother's wombs like St. Joseph, but we have been baptized. Through our baptism, we were regenerated and given the graces

---

3   The great early Church Doctors, including St. Jerome and St. Athanasius, taught that St. Joseph was a young man and he lived and died *as a virgin*! He is also presented as young in ancient Christian artwork. It seems the notion that he was an older man stems from a second-century apocryphal document going by the name of *Protoevangelium of James*. While that work contains some edifying and legitimate traditions, it was also condemned on account of errors and thus *explicitly* rejected as a candidate for the canon of Scripture. It is quite likely that the *Protoevangelium* sought to present Joseph as older in order to safeguard Mary's perpetual virginity. It claimed that the *brethren of the Lord* referred to in Scripture were Joseph's children from a prior marriage. However, this argument runs contrary to the more ancient traditions that these "brethren" were members of Our Lord's extended family. The notion that Joseph was an older man is not held by the Church Fathers, makes far less sense theologically, and demonstrates less reverent piety toward St. Joseph. Sadly, it gained wider acceptance in the East and has become more popular today.

necessary to live a life of virtue and perfection. St. Joseph cooperated with the graces bestowed on him by God, and his love of poverty forged a character more ironclad than any man on earth. The daily renunciation of earthly pleasures was a norm for St. Joseph. He entered into a special marriage with Mary already having cultivated his chastity through a supernatural love of poverty.

Our culture desires that men be effeminate: soft, inconstant, pleasure-seeking, and useless. In order to obtain a level of virtue worthy of heaven, we must learn to love poverty. By giving away our resources to others, we will build a greater trust in God's providence. By rejecting common comforts, we will strengthen our resolve against the temptations of the flesh.

Seek to love poverty like St. Joseph. Start by praying to him every day for this grace. Be heroic in your generosity, and deny yourself daily. An excellent form of self-denial is fasting from entertainment and sports. Instead, one can spend more time as a father teaching and interacting with one's children or in acts of service for one's wife that serve the family's greater good. Make the effort to fast from food and technology. Reject the constant consumption of more. These things may be difficult, but precisely because of that, they will go a long way toward helping men be less effeminate.

Remember, the Holy Family celebrated the first Christmas in a cave; therefore, let us also seek greater poverty in the very foundation of our life.

St. Joseph, Lover of Poverty, pray for us!

St. Joseph, Pillar of Families

When we meditate upon the infancy narrative, we find Joseph seemingly distressed at the revelation of Mary's pregnancy through the Holy Ghost. Unfortunately, many modern commentators present Joseph as a noble yet hurt and confused man. They tend to present him as troubled by the news of Our Lady's pregnancy: he doesn't wish to hurt Mary's reputation as a fiancé engaged to him but pregnant out of wedlock and not by him. Like much of the modern trends in biblical scholarship, this interpretation is sheer nonsense.

At this point, Mary and Joseph were already married in accordance with traditional Hebrew custom. To consider them merely engaged is an anachronistic misunderstanding based upon our societal conventions. In the time of Christ, Jewish couples would go through a two-stage marriage process. The first would be what we might call betrothal, and the second would be in accordance with tradition's use of the term *consummation*. An important distinction is that the first step was public and already entailed the commitment of both. It was common for a couple to go through the first stage while the husband would spend time building a home for the expected consummation and beginning of family life.

In Matthew 1:18, we learn that "Mary was espoused to Joseph, but before they came together, She was found with Child, of the Holy Ghost." To suggest that Mary was something like an unwed mother is not only erroneous but rude and even sacrilegious against Our Lady's immaculate purity. In the next verse, we see that Joseph was "a just man, and not willing to publicly expose her" (v. 19). When the Holy Bible calls a man just, it is a reference to his religiosity, piety, and virtue. Joseph was a magnificently devout man, and his marriage to Mary followed the proper stages. His hesitancy to bring his legal and legitimate wife into his home was not because of any public perception, or because there might be talk, or because he suspected violations of the sixth commandment. There is no allusion in the Holy Bible to any such thing. Rather, it is because of his great and perfect humility. Consider the context! What the Holy Bible does say is that St. Joseph is just. The reference is thus to his relationship with God and how well he lived out Our Lord's exhortation to "be perfect as your heavenly Father is perfect" (Mt. 5:48).

Joseph knew who Mary was. He may not have known that she was the Immaculate Conception, but he knew that she was holier than anyone else he had ever known.[4] He had never known her to have sinned. He knew she had lived a life consecrated to God in the Temple since she was three. He knew she was unlike any other woman in the world.[5]

---

4   Have you ever met someone who is very pure and innocent? A certain beauty radiates from that person. We sometimes get a glimpse of this in those religious who consecrate themselves to God. Yet the Blessed Virgin Mary far exceeds the purity, innocence, and perfection of anyone we may ever know on this earth. That kind of sanctity is in some way visible and palpable to all, yet even more so to those who are *just*.

5   I once heard a sermon in which the heretical statement was made that Our Lady was an ordinary fourteen-year-old girl whom God "happened to choose." Nothing could be further from the truth. No one who knew Our Lady would have ever described her as "an ordinary girl." Could you see yourself describing a perfectly sinless person as "oh yeah, she's just like the girl next door"? These kinds

He may not have known every detail of things yet revealed, but he knew that a Virgin would bring forth the Messiah. He knew of his family lineage through the House of David, and he knew the arrival of the fulfillment of the prophecies of the Old Testament was at hand.

Upon hearing of Mary's miraculous conception, Joseph would not have doubted her truthfulness. He knew she was with Child by the power of the Holy Ghost, and the weight of this responsibility was immeasurable. Beholding Our Lady's purity, her unparalleled beauty, and now being aware of her heavenly royalty, the humble St. Joseph did not consider himself worthy of her. In true humility, he saw himself not befitting of such a role, as it was divine in origin. Like St. Padre Pio, who felt unworthy of the stigmata, St. Joseph loved God so much that he couldn't view himself as having lordship in a fatherly way over his Lord and God.

St. Joseph was only able to overcome his humble sense of unworthiness by a miracle—an outpouring of God's grace. Namely, God sent an angel to tell St. Joseph not to be afraid and to let him know it was the divine will that he be the husband and protector of Our Lady. Filled with wisdom and prudence, St. Joseph rightly discerned that the angel indeed brought a message from God. Then, always being perfectly obedient to God, he joyfully and promptly cooperated with the unique grace received (see Mt. 1:20–24).

Upon his change of heart and acceptance of the task, St. Joseph became the patriarch of the Holy Family.

of heretical and sacrilegious statements only come from the mouths of those who do not know Our Lady and who lack piety.

Throughout those unseen years of Christ's youth, it was
Joseph who built and guided a family worthy of the Son
of God. Jesus, the Son of the carpenter, was apprenticed to
Joseph and, in his human nature, became an image of his
earthly father in the same way that we all resemble our own
fathers. Jesus Our Lord kept the commandments; therefore,
he honored his father and his mother. What a mountain of a
man Joseph must have been to deserve the honorable obedience of our Savior!

Furthermore, the concrete fortitude of Joseph's countenance must have been unmatched. It is hard enough for
the average man to handle the stress of running a normal
household, with normal children. Yet somehow St. Joseph
could withstand the weight and power of the Creator of
heaven and earth living with him, looking up to him with
the eyes of a child. It sends shivers down my spine to think
what the childlike gaze of Jesus Christ would have felt like
as he looked up at St. Joseph, lifting up his arms in the
motion that all children do when they want their father to
hold them.

As if the weight of raising the Second Person of the
Holy Trinity wasn't enough, Joseph also gave our Blessed
Mother the love, respect, and protection befitting of the
Immaculate Conception. What an awesome responsibility
to have to be the head of one who is perfected in grace.[6] Yet
the Pillar of Families gave the Mystical Rose a home life

---

6   When one meditates upon this reality, it makes complete theologi-
     cal sense that St. Joseph must also have been personally sinless. If
     he had suffered any actual sin, he would not have been able to be
     the head of the Holy Family, guiding and directing both Our Lady
     and Our Lord. Pious tradition holds that St. Joseph was sanctified

befitting of the New Eve. No matter the material poverty, Joseph himself became the pillar and bulwark of the new Eden requisite for the long-awaited woman prophesied in Genesis 3:15.

The mystery of St. Joseph's majesty is endless. In these times of terrible confusion about family and fatherhood in our decaying society, let us look to St. Joseph. All men must strive to foster a pious and fervent devotion to him. How else do we expect to lead our families well? Beg him for the grace to imitate him, to have a holy headship over your family. This, too, is an awesome responsibility, yet God has entrusted it to you.

As Christ himself looked to Joseph, carrying heavy loads of wood on his shoulders from forest to workshop, let us look to the man who showed the Child Jesus how to carry his forthcoming cross for inspiration to carry ours.

St. Joseph, Pillar of Families, pray for us!

St. Joseph, Chaste Guardian of the Virgin

When we consider the journey of the Blessed Mother and St. Joseph to Bethlehem, traditionally there are two common theories pertaining to the route that Joseph and Mary may have taken. The first is sometimes called the trade route, and it is the shortest. This route goes through Samaritan territory and is technically a shorter route; however, it is more undulated in terrain. Furthermore, the tension between the Jews and Samaritans was highly contentious, which meant that traveling along this route would present clear dangers

---

within his mother's womb, not at conception, but certainly by the time he was born. Thereafter, he never committed a sin.

for the Holy Family. The second route is known as the Jordan Valley route due to the fact that it crosses the valley that bears that name. It is geographically a longer route, but it is generally flatter and was not as distinctly hostile of an environment as regards the Jew-Samaritan conflict, although it did present its own dangers.

It is reasonable to believe that the Holy Family chose the second route, even though it, too, was dangerous. This route also took Mary and Joseph past or through Jericho, which seems in continuity with the parable of the Good Samaritan.

Joseph was tasked with protecting and transporting the Blessed Mother from Nazareth to Bethlehem for the census called by Caesar Augustus. While we cannot be sure how the Blessed Mother experienced pain, due to her special redemption and perfection, it is reasonable to assume that a journey such as this would present discomfort.[7] She was very far along in her virginal pregnancy, and the journey would take place on the back of a beast of burden.

The Jordan Valley is the lowest place on earth and is the location of the Dead Sea. Our Lady, led by St. Joseph, carried Our Lord by the lifeless waters of the pit of the earth. This route also took the Holy Family to Jericho, a place

---

7   It is a clear teaching of tradition that Our Lady did not experience labor pains because those specific pains are part of the curse from original sin (see Gen. 3:16). It is in effect heretical to suggest that Our Lady would have had labor pains, for it is an implicit denial of Her *Immaculate Conception*. However, many mystics, such as Ven. Mary of Agreda, indicate that, in general, Our Lord and Our Lady experienced greater physical, mental, and spiritual pains than the rest of us on account of their perfect integrity.

known for being rife with robbers and murderers looking to exploit the innocence of vulnerable travelers. In a sense, this road to Bethlehem prefigured what Our Lord would go through on his road to the cross.

St. Joseph guarded the Most Holy Virgin through this land of death. Envision the criminal threat present around every corner, especially given the shorter days and darker evenings of the winter season. St. Joseph was perfectly aware of the spiritual forces that writhed in pain at the virginal monstrance of Our Lady's womb. The priest of the Holy Family processed his wife and unborn Son through the valley of death. It is here that King David's words come alive: "For though I should walk in the midst of the shadow of death, I will fear no evils, for thou art with me. Thy rod and thy staff, they have comforted me" (Ps. 22:4). Perhaps Mary contemplated these words, rubbing her womb the way expectant mothers are wont to do, as she gazed lovingly at her husband, finding comfort in his masculine countenance, strength, and noble courage.

With each dominating footstep, St. Joseph sent a warning to the depths of hell that the coming of Christ was approaching. Through the dark of night, he led the chariot of Our Lady, her perfect holiness lighting the way while Joseph marched his family forward through the descending fog of demons. This chaste guardian of the Virgin was not a diminutive man but a conqueror, flanked by the Prince of the Heavenly Host and his angels. Venerable Mary of Agreda relates the following: "They were accompanied by angels, who were appointed by God Himself, as the servants of Her Majesty during that whole journey. These heavenly squadrons marched along as their retinue in human forms visible to the heavenly Lady."

At the end of every valley, there is an ascent to be made to climb upwards out of the deep. As they passed by the degenerate city of Jericho, they began their ascent out of the valley of death. This was the hardest part of the journey, a steep climb after days of exhaustive trekking through unforgiving weather and terrain. From the Limbo of the Fathers, Adam, Noah, Abraham, Moses, and David watched as the Light of the Patriarchs showed them the glory soon to come when Christ would descend to the dead in order to raise the holy men of old from the shadows.[8]

---

8   We can extend this typology of the Holy Family even further. From Jericho, they would ascend all the way to Jerusalem on Mount Zion, which serves as an image of the Resurrection, for Jerusalem prefigures the heavenly city of God. The Church Fathers teach that in the parable of the Good Samaritan, the man who descends from Jerusalem to Jericho is fallen man in the person of Adam. The thieves that waylay him are Satan and his demons. Even prior to his physical birth, we already see the new Adam reversing, or undoing, this original fall. From Jerusalem, the Holy Family made the short six-mile journey to Bethlehem. Bethlehem means "House of Bread," and it is our resurrected Lord who makes himself *really present* to us in the Holy Eucharist. In those days, St. Joseph and Our Lady placed him in a manger, the feedbox of animals, and now we, his sheep, come to his house (his churches) to be fed the Bread of Eternal Life. Bethlehem is also the City of David, from whence comes the King who shall rule forever. This evokes Christ's social kingship, so neglected today, and his eternal reign which shall be ushered by his second coming. Thus, in a mystical sense, the Holy Family's journey from Nazareth to Bethlehem prefigures Our Lord's great paschal mystery, from infancy to passion and cross to resurrection and even to his eternal reign.

We all stand on the shoulders of giants, men who have gone before us to forge our path. Even Jesus Christ, in his human nature, had an example to follow in St. Joseph. Before Christ's ascent up to Calvary came Joseph's journey to Bethlehem. Let us not forget to fall in line behind the guardian of Christ and Mary, as we too climb through the valley of death so as to adore the Savior and kneel at the communion rail to receive the King of Kings!

St. Joseph, Chaste Guardian of the Virgin, pray for us!

St. Joseph, Watchful Defender of Christ

Every father has at one time or another laid awake in the early hours of the morning worrying about his family. These worries may be financial, health-related, moral, spiritual, or even related to the safety of your family. In reality, most often fathers worry about a combination of these things. Being a father is a lot like being a military general. We are tasked with a great responsibility that includes everything from assessing potential threats to maintaining the morale of those we have sworn to protect. In our society today, reasons to worry are everywhere. It is difficult to even take your children into a grocery store, as immoral magazine covers are displayed right beside the register at the eye level of a child. In any case, fathers must keep watch if they are to defend their children, whatever the threat may be. Fortunately, we have a model to look to! "And after they were departed, behold an angel of the Lord appeared in sleep to Joseph, saying: Arise, and take the Child and His Mother, and fly into Egypt: and be there until I shall tell thee. For it will come to pass that Herod will seek the child to destroy him. Who arose, and took the child and his mother by night, and retired into Egypt: and he was there until the death of Herod" (Mt. 2:13–14).

This account of the Holy Family's escape from Herod and the slaughter of the Holy Innocents is commonly meditated upon as one of the Seven Sorrows of Mary. Very soon after the Nativity, Our Lady distinctly felt the sorrow she would experience by bringing Christ into the world. Alongside our Blessed Mother was St. Joseph. We see the urgency in the departure as Joseph took Jesus and Mary away *by night*. Traveling by night is not ideal, and a father would only lead his family away under the cover of darkness if the threat required such a bold and expedient response.[9]

Not only did Joseph take his newly established Holy Family away from their home, but he took them all the way to Egypt. The situation was so severe in Israel that the watchful defender of Christ had to take the King of the Jews to the principality of Pharaoh. How great the threat against Christ must have been for Joseph to take his family away from Israel, the world's only haven for the Jews, to Egypt, a pagan and hostile land.

But is this not the world we all live in now? As fathers, are we not required to remain watchful as we navigate our families through the wasteland of a morally bankrupt civilization? Our current society is as much an anti-Christian

---

9   Tradition holds that the soldiers sought Jesus among his relatives, including Zachary and Elizabeth. Elizabeth fled into the desert with the young John the Baptist, but Zachary gave his life in order for them to escape. Herod's soldiers murdered Zachary for refusing to reveal where Jesus and his own son were.

wasteland as there has ever been. In fact, it is as if our culture seeks to worship all the same demons that held sway in Ancient Egypt. Idolatry and the violation of the first three commandments, which govern man's relationship with God, have become socially institutionalized.

The relationship that children form with their father serves as a natural foundation upon which they build their relationship with God the Father. When children do not see their father as good, loving, forgiving, protecting, selfless, or watching out for their best interests, it is that much more difficult for them to believe God the Father has these qualities. Yet when children have strong and healthy relationships with their human fathers, it is far easier for them to believe that God the Father is all-good, all-merciful, and directs all things toward our growth in grace and our salvation. There is a direct correlation between our society's descent into paganism and the great loss of Christian fatherhood.

As a sinless and perfect foster father, St. Joseph served the Christ Child as the model par excellence of the perfect heavenly Father. Let us beg St. Joseph's intercession for the grace to imitate him as exemplary fathers who strive to help our children form relationships of faith, hope, and charity with our heavenly Father.

Like St. Joseph, fathers are called to protect their families. Many men take seriously the need to physically protect their families, but spiritual protection is likewise the role of the father. In fact, it is even more important. When fathers are absent from their families, be it physically, excessively withdrawn, or spiritually truant, there is a terrible void that leads to a host of temptations and opens a door to many evils. We must examine our conscience on these matters, consider well how we can improve, and then develop a plan of action in which we persevere.

The time for men to truly be men is long overdue. No longer can we sit back and watch the culture assault our families. It is not enough for us to take a passive approach to the threats that seek the ruin of our souls. Instead, we must form plans and set goals to help us be good fathers— and pray for the grace to persevere in these resolutions. We must stand watch at all hours of the night and prepare to defend our kin the way St. Joseph defended Our Lord and Our Lady.

St. Joseph, Watchful Defender of Christ, pray for us!

St. Joseph, Head of the Holy Family

The man's headship in the family, as I have discussed, is perhaps one of the most contentious issues among even faithful Catholics today. It is such a stumbling block for women—and even men—that many priests try to skirt the issue whenever the words "Wives, be subject to your husbands, as it behoveth in the Lord" (Col. 3:18) come up in the lessons for the sacred liturgy. Our society is patently antipathetic toward the traditional role of the husband as the head of the household. It is easy enough to understand how the various toxic philosophies so rampant today have brought disorder into the home. However, many do not stop to consider how this lack of male headship creates a vacuum, which either the woman or no one will properly fill.

Headship of a family is built into the very nature of a man, and when he fails at this task, it affects the health of his whole family and, consequently, all of society. Wives who are not led and served by a loving and self-sacrificing husband are not secure. Daughters who cannot look to a father who is on a mission to sanctify his family will encounter difficulty in understanding their worth as a child of God the Father. Furthermore, sons in this situation will be stunted in their development as men, which means they will have to work so much harder to reorder things correctly when they have their own families.

We can be certain that St. Joseph showed proper headship of the Holy Family. He demonstrated this on many occasions, not least of which in his role as Pillar of Families and Chaste Guardian of the Virgin. Men today need not only an example of headship but also an example of how to become a man who is ready for the role. We all need to be freed from the bondage by which a world opposed to God envelopes us.[10]

Men should not be surprised when they encounter resistance to God's established order and their headship within their own household. However, before being enraged by the specks of dust in the eyes of their wives and children, men should strive to remove the beams of wood from their own eye (see Mt. 7:5). It is futile to try and force one's family to accept the proper order of things when one is himself not properly ordered. In fact, precisely because the man is

---

10   Recall the words from the last Gospel of the Mass: "He was in the world, and the world was made by him, and the world knew him not. He came unto his own, and his own received him not" (Jn. 1:10–11). This opposition of the world to God has been greatly intensified in modern times by our secular, hedonistic, and atheistic society.

the head of the family, he naturally sets the example for those under his authority to follow.

A man should realize that, in general, his family will reject his authority to the degree with which he himself rejects God's authority. It is often even to a greater degree on account of our fallen nature. For example, consider how readily children amplify the faults of their parents. If you have long lived a worldly life with disorder in the roots of your interior life and within the fabric of your home, it will be humanly impossible for you to right the ship. I say humanly impossible, but nothing is impossible with God's grace and guidance.

When Moses went up the mountain to receive the Ten Commandments, we read in the Holy Bible that the people "rose up to play" (Ex. 32:6), meaning ritual debauchery. Aaron was the weak man who had not truly left Egypt, whereas Moses was the man of God who had thoroughly rejected Egypt. It cannot be overemphasized: just as the Hebrews who went out of Egypt retained many pagan ideas and desires, so too many Catholics cling to the Egypt within their souls. Every step we take toward emptying our hearts of worldly desires—of the world's false maxims, vanities, and fleeting pleasures—is a step we can then take toward God. Yet, if our heart is filled with love of transitory things, there will be no room in it for love of the eternal. In this we must imitate Moses, not Aaron.

We should, however, not make the error of thinking that Aaron was a "kind and understanding" leader, having compassion for the people's weaknesses (sin!), whereas Moses was strict and uncaring. Aaron actually tries to excuse his grievous sin by blaming the people and speaks as if he had no role in calling for gold and fashioning the idolatrous calf (Ex. 32:2–4). Instead, he implies that the calf spontaneously emerged from the fire (see v. 24).

Moses, on the other hand, intercedes for the people and begs God to forgive them. God threatens to wipe them from the face of the earth, and Moses pleads to God that he may have mercy on them for his own name's sake (see v. 11–13). Moses then freely offers himself as a reparatory sacrifice to God, accepting the people's sin as his own and asking God to punish him instead (see v. 31–32).

Moses clearly serves as a prefigurement for Christ, whereas Aaron acts as an imitator of Adam. These are the two choices constantly before every man: to act like the old Adam or like the new Adam. Do you excuse your own sin and blame those under you, deluding yourself that you are kind and compassionate? Or do you faithfully adhere to God's ways, accept responsibility for the sins of those under you, and offer yourself as a sacrifice, willingly accepting the just punishments for their sins? Herein we see the mark of a real man who truly serves and leads as head of his family according to God's right order.

This reality lies at the essence of priesthood: to willingly offer himself in sacrifice on behalf of his people. Every husband and father is called to live thus for his family. Even more so is every Catholic priest ordained for this role; the bishop is called to heroically live this for his diocesan flock; above all, the pope ought to exemplify this most perfectly as Christ's vicar on earth.

In order to become the domestic priests we are called to be, we need to follow Moses's example. Yet before we can willingly offer ourselves in reparatory sacrifice, we must spend time in the desert. This means that we need to embrace ascetical practices in an intentional way.

If we are to rid our souls of Egypt and become men fashioned after the model of Moses and St. Joseph, then we must begin our Exodus from effeminacy immediately. Do not hesitate to challenge yourself! With God's grace, every man is capable of achieving great virtue and recapturing the proper spiritual and moral headship over himself and his family.

St. Joseph, Head of the Holy Family, pray for us!

St. Joseph, Glory of Domestic Life

To say that St. Joseph is the Glory of Domestic Life is to say that in him we see a supreme example of how a man magnificently transforms home life. There is a certain splendor, even honor, in the household when it is properly ordered and guided by the fatherly example of St. Joseph.

For many men, and even many women, domestic life is a secondary consideration. Our main focus is often our workplace, a place at which men increasingly spend more time than they should. Most women today work outside the home, which has never been the Church's understanding of the feminine role.

Due to the absence of both father and mother in the home, families are increasingly isolated from one another and parents rely on institutions to care for and, in many respects, raise their children. In our society, many children begin to spend the majority of their time away from their mother and father as infants. If you consider day care, babysitting, school, clubs, lessons, and extracurricular activities, most North American children spend perhaps three to five hours per day around their parents. Furthermore, much of this scant time spent among family will be in the car and, regrettably, in front of personal media devices. In better scenarios, mothers will stay home, and even if the children go off to school, they will have spent their formative early years with their mother. In addition, with their mother at home, children will spend only a few hours away rather than the length of an extensive work day, filling time with after school programs and day care. Now, even if children are fortunate enough to have their mother in the home, this does not mean that it is acceptable for the father to be continually absent.

On the topic of the duties of a husband, the *Roman Catechism* states, "The husband should also be constantly occupied in some honest pursuit with a view to provide necessaries for the support of his family and to avoid idleness, the root of almost every vice." Many Catholic men understand this, and they do work hard to provide the material necessities for their loved ones.

However, the *Roman Catechism* goes on to say, "He is also to keep all his family in order, to correct their morals, and see that they faithfully discharge their duties."[11] Husbands are required to ensure that the moral and domestic framework of a home is in proper order. How can a father ensure this if he spends most of his time away from the home? In a word, he can't.

---

11   *The Catechism of the Council of Trent* (Gastonia, NC: TAN Books, 2009), p. 377.

It is understandable that these teachings may seem paradoxical, especially in today's industrialized society. It is true that many men have to commute to work and that many places of employment are not overly concerned with ample leisure and family time. The state of our materialistic society is truly regrettable, and husbands who are stuck between the proverbial rock and a hard place should not feel ashamed if, even while doing their best, a work-life balance is difficult. We must use our prudential judgment, but it is objectively better for a mother to be home with the children, even if the husband has to work harder, than it is for children to rarely see both father and mother.

Now, "no word shall be impossible with God" (Luke 1:37). Holy Mother Church never instructs us to accomplish something that is unattainable, even if the task seems impossible by worldly standards. We do not operate by mere material and earthly means but instead we rely on grace to perfect nature and the supernatural to transform the natural. St. Joseph shows us how a modest life of a craftsman can provide the commensurate glory due to the King of Kings and the Queen of Heaven. If we follow his model, we see that we can find a way to blend our work and home life into a single organism, something that moves with and for the rhythms of domestic life.

Our faith is a faith of sacrifice, and St. Joseph shows us that saying yes to a seemingly impossible task is a demonstration of how God's generosity will provide even in the direst of circumstances. Imagine if St. Joseph looked with worldly eyes at the circumstances of the Nativity. Only a man of unmatchable faith could see with God's eyes the glory of the birth of Christ in a den of animal husbandry.

We must ask ourselves what sacrifices we can make as fathers in order to spend more time with our families. Do we really need all that living space? Could our family do with one car? Can we take less expensive vacations? Might our children not do better with less toys, clothes, and entertainment? I am sure that, in most cases, we can find ways to reorient our money and abstain from costly habits in order to maximize our resources.

My wife and I recently spent time with beloved friends of ours who raised eleven children in a downtown three-bedroom home on very modest means. The father trusted God in his career and was able to cultivate a work-home balance that allowed him to spend significant time with his family. Most people would call this situation unreal or crazy, but it is the world that has gone insane. The heroic virtue this man displayed actually created a properly ordered Christian home, which is further evidenced by the complementary relationship between husband and wife and their rightly understood Christian marriage. The joy in a home like this is contagious, it is palpable, and it contradicts every worldly understanding of domestic life. Families like this help to remedy a world that has dispensed with God in the pursuit of disposable idols.

Each home life will look different, and no two situations are exactly the same. But if we are honest with ourselves, I suspect we can make more and greater sacrifices for the good of our family life. I imagine we can be more generous with God, who will never be outdone in providing for his children. If we ask our Father for bread, he will never give us a stone. Let us never forget that God will never be outdone—by anyone—in generosity!

I encourage husbands to consult with their wives and evaluate the material situation of their life. Pinpoint areas that can be changed, and readjust financial expectations in order to give more glory to God by following the domestic example of St. Joseph. As strange as our world economy can be, with the advent of information technology, there are unique ways we can seek to work from home, or even transfer our professional skills into a family business. In some cases, perhaps we should even rethink our line of work, after much prayer and consultation with a holy priest. Ultimately, we should seek to do God's will, which, as St. Joseph shows us, might result in interesting surprises.[12]

In the meantime, I recommend the following prayer for gainful employment, which also can be said by those who are already employed but hope to provide in a more family-oriented way:

> Dear St. Joseph, you were yourself once faced with the responsibility of providing the necessities of life for Jesus and Mary. Look down with fatherly compassion upon me in my anxiety over my present inability to support my family. Please help me to find gainful employment very soon, so that this heavy burden of concern will be lifted from my heart and that I am soon able to provide for those whom God has entrusted to my care. Help us to guard against bitterness and discouragement, so that we may emerge from this trial spiritually enriched and with even greater blessings from God. Amen
>
> St. Joseph, Glory of Domestic Life, pray for us!

---

12 See the website for more practical information about the crucial topic of finances: https://www.meaningofcatholic.com/terrorof demons/.

St. Joseph, Most Valiant

To be valiant is to demonstrate valor. Valor is defined as a demonstration of great courage, especially in battle. Often when we think of St. Joseph, we envision a mild, perhaps even elderly man. This view may be the influence of certain artwork. Unfortunately, this timid presentation of Joseph does not help, and in some ways does harm to our understanding of St. Joseph as the warrior of the Holy Family.

There is no mention of St. Joseph in the Holy Bible that alludes to him participating in any physical battle; thus, we can assume that the title of Valiant may be applied to another sort of battle. Surely it is believable that St. Joseph was a physically competent man, and due to his skills as a craftsman, it is certain that he could have swung a sword like he did an ax. However, our battles in the Christian life, although at times manifested in our material nature, take place on the spiritual plain with constant ferocity. "For our wrestling is not against flesh and blood; but against principalities and powers, against the rulers of the world of this darkness, against the spirits of wickedness in the high places" (Eph. 6:12).

Our ultimate battle is against Satan, and in our day, the demon is relentless in his hatred of the human race. The ancient dragon tirelessly seeks to poison the well of divine life by using every method he can to spread spiritual and moral disease into the heart of every family. Sister Lucia, before her death, rightly prophesied that the final battle for souls would take place in marriage and the family.[13]

---

13 Karl Marx infamously claimed in his *Communists Manifesto* that for socialism to succeed, three things must be destroyed: property, religion, and *the family*.

We need not dive into the tragedy that is the state of marriage and family in the twenty-first century, but needless to say, it is bleak.[14] We have all been touched, directly or indirectly, by the deluge of disorder that enwraps the very underpinnings of society. We are correct in taking the aforementioned words of St. Paul to heart, and we must believe that the greatest theater of battle is in fact on the plains of prayer. Souls living in a state of grace, mothers tenderly caring for their children, and fathers resting on bended knee are like unyielding crusaders against the devils. Furthermore, St. Paul tells us in the next verse that we must put on the armor of God. This requires us to cover ourselves in divine help, with the sacraments as our artillery against the wickedness and snares of the devil.

Fortunately, we can look to the Most Valiant St. Joseph as our guide. Christian men have been fooled in our time, and our interior lives have become soft and flabby. Too often we see prayer as a feminine pursuit, and for some reason, it seems as if we have dispensed with any manly form of piety.[15]

---

14   Consider the following quote by Fr. Vincent Miceli in *The Antichrist* (Ignatius Press, 1981): "Satan, his demons and their human henchmen know that the fate of mankind depends on the spiritual durability of family relationships. If one splits the atom [the basic building block of molecules], tremendous physical disaster results from the explosive forces released. [Likewise,] if one splits the [nuclear] family, the basic building block of society, tremendous disaster results from the explosive passions released. There is no law against splitting the atom. But God Himself forbids splitting the family. *What God has joined together, let no man put asunder*."

15   Various reasons have been put forth as to why men seem less inclined to piety. In my opinion, two of the most convincing are

Men are often called to be vulnerable in the spiritual life, but is this a good thing? Yes, it is a good thing if by vulnerable we mean that a man lays himself down in front of the Lord to be molded like iron, beaten and chastised into a perfected form.

We often hear of God as Father, but what does this fatherhood look like? We should look to St. Joseph, the earthly example of the fatherhood to which Christ subjected himself. We should expect to find austerity and discipline in this father-Son relationship. St. Joseph, in a way, shows us God the Father in how he raises Christ. The greatest of human virtues are habitually present in St. Joseph's daily life. It is no accident that St. Joseph demonstrated so high a degree of valor. God the Father selected a human foster father who, in even the smallest minutiae of life, modeled patience in trials and redemptive suffering in the most exemplary manner. One would expect nothing less from the household in which Christ grew up; after all, is there any greater act of valor than the passion of Christ?

---

the following. (1) Anthropological. By nature, a man is the initiator and he gives, while a woman, on the other hand, is receptive. She receives and then takes what is given so as to nurture life within her. In the spiritual life, it is God who is the initiator, and he gives his grace. The human must receive what God gives and nurture that within his soul so that the spiritual life will flourish. Thus, the religious life comes naturally to a woman, but not so to the man. (2) Men want to be challenged and exert themselves so as to master difficult things. Since Vatican II, the Catholic faith has largely been watered-down, diluted, and weakened. Gone are the exhortations to the ascetic life. It has become very effeminate. Thus, many Catholic men have been repulsed by how the Faith is being practiced in most parishes.

In addition, we hear of having a relationship with Jesus Christ. This is, of course, a wonderful thing, but of what does this relationship consist? As men, if we truly have a relationship with Christ, the King of heaven, then we have a relationship with a conqueror. Christ's entrance into the world and later descent into the hell of the just (after dying on the cross) were not delicate affairs. He broke down the fortress of Satan and conquered death itself. The name of Our Lord strikes immeasurable fear into the hearts of demons. It is St. Joseph who humbly accepted his fatherly role, tasked with forming the Valiant Victor of the Crucifixion. Our relationship with Christ is a relationship with a God of victory, a Lord who desires only valiant men at his pierced side. "The Lord is as a Man of War" (Ex. 15:2).

Examine your life. Does your virtue approach the standard needed to habituate the valor required of heaven? Is your prayer an exercise in self-comfort, or is it a training ground for war? Our Church needs men of valor more than she ever has before. For too long have our swords been sheathed, watching as the enemy parades in and out of our families, stealing innocence and life. We must say *no more* to this satanic saturation of our formerly Christian society. It is time for valiant men to model St. Joseph and march toward this den of thieves. Unleash the power of the Rosary and marvel at the graceful destruction Our Lady levels against Lucifer and his legions. Onward, Christian soldiers, the time for valor has come.

St. Joseph, Most Valiant, pray for us!

St. Joseph, Model of Workmen

This is St. Joseph's workshop — old and quaint!
So we will enter for a little space,
And watch with loving eyes our favourite Saint,
As to and fro he moves about the place.
His placid brow no trace of care betrays,
A heavenly look of peace is resting there,
How calm his face — how self-controlled his ways!
His very attitude suggests a prayer.[16]

At the beginning of time, "the Lord God took man, and put him into the paradise of pleasure, to dress it, and to keep it" (Gen. 2:15). In part, Adam was created to work, to participate in the creativity of God through stewardship of the gifts bestowed on mankind by our Creator. In essence, Adam was a gardener; therefore, work in the truest sense was ordained to be a blessing.

Nevertheless, at the Fall, God tells Adam: "Cursed is the earth in thy work; with labour and toil shalt thou eat thereof all the days of thy life. Thorns and thistles shall it bring forth to thee; and thou shalt eat the herbs of the earth. In the sweat of thy face shalt thou eat bread till thou return to the earth, out of which thou wast taken: for dust thou art, and into dust thou shalt return" (Gen. 3:17–19).

What we see here is that Adam's work now entails punishment. Clearly, work itself is not evil, for God created Adam to work in the Garden of Eden before the Fall. However, having sinned mortally, Adam thus cut himself off

---

16 Taken from a poem called "St. Joseph's Workshop," from a book called *St. Joseph of Jesus and Mary* by Rev. Matther Russell, SJ, 1898.

from the divine life. Man's work—apart from God—has now become a curse.

It is true that God may confer punishments primarily to apply divine justice, but there is always a corrective element in God's punishments and chastisements, which is intended to bring about great good. Depending on the gravity and frequency of sin, God, in his infinite wisdom, will calibrate punishments accurately. With God, the punishment always fits the crime, and the punishment even serves to correct the root causes of the sin. In the case of Adam, the punishment is severe due to Adam's clear knowledge of God before the Fall, but it is also a corrective path of redemption for man. In this punishment, we see hints of the coming of Christ and his passion and death regarding the thorns and sweat.

Salvation is a process and, throughout thousands of years, the Israelites worked through the ripple effect that emanates from the original sin. Throughout these unseen years, men had to navigate through the curse of Adam as they grappled with the paradoxical combination of both the dignity and the suffering of daily work. We can all relate to the fact that while working is good for the soul, it is also a cause of great stress or hardship. Even if we have jobs that are fulfilling, there will always be moments of displeasure and anxiety.

Since work is a tool of corrective punishment, we must approach our obligations with the proper disposition. If we view our daily tasks as meaningless unpleasantries, then doubtless we will become bitter and fail to cultivate any virtue. On the contrary, if we resolve to be sanctified through our jobs, we will develop an honorable Christian character.

Since we are to *pray without ceasing*, we must somehow incorporate prayer into our daily work in order to achieve this mandate. But how is it that we can do this? It cannot be that we must, for example, recite Rosaries all day, something practically impossible. In addition, some jobs require great mental acuity and therefore great focus on a particular task, rendering the contemplation of God by man impossible.

The answer to this challenge of unceasing prayer is to make your work a prayer. To do this, one should consciously offer up his labor to God. Do this every day—for example, with a Morning Offering. One should also labor with the right intention—namely, the glory of God, the salvation of one's soul, and the fulfillment of the duties of one's state in life. It is also of great advantage to offer brief prayers throughout the workday. These can take a second, such as "Jesus, have mercy," or "St. Joseph, pray for me," or any of the Fatima prayers of reparation.[17] Naturally, one would make every effort to ensure that his labor is not a cause for sin and would even avoid (flee from) the temptations that his labor might present. Yet without sanctifying

---

17 Along with a virtuous work ethic, it is also possible to insert some prayer into your work day. The Angelus is a perfect prayer to insert at your lunch hour. Decades of the Rosary can be prayed throughout the day, and visible sacred symbols keep our minds focused on God. There is an old tradition of Catholics praying one Hail Mary at the beginning of the hour, a way of blessing their time; all of us could do this.

grace, daily meditation, and a recollected spirit, it is impossible for man to fulfill St. Paul's exhortation.

Fortunately, God has provided St. Joseph as the perfect model for us to follow in this pursuit:

> See how unceasingly he plies his trade;
> His heavy saw is heard from hour to hour.
> St. Joseph's work went well because he prayed:
> Here is a lesson — Prayer gives work its power!
> Labour and prayer his twin companions are.
> And they are comrades also to us given:
> Will they not sanctify, and lift us far
> Above the snares that line our path to heaven?

A prayerful work ethic is a great bulwark against complacency and idleness. No matter our jobs, we will spend many of our waking hours working. We must seek ways to make holy our work days in order that our sinful inclinations be perfected. Finally, in our culture that is increasingly hostile to the Gospel, a truly masculine Catholic man can make Christ known through the way he carries himself at work. Our actions and performance may be the only gospel our coworkers have ever seen.

Here is a prayer from the *Raccolta* (No. 478) that one can pray each day before starting work.

> O Glorious St. Joseph, pattern of all who are devoted to labour, obtain for me the grace to labour in the spirit of penance, in order thereby to atone for my many sins; to labour conscientiously, putting devotion to duty before my own inclinations; to labour with thankfulness and joy, deeming it an honour to employ and to develop, by my labour, the gifts I have received from Almighty God; to work with order, peace, moderation, and patience, without ever shrinking from weariness and difficulties; to work above all with a pure intention and with detachment from

self, having always before my eyes the hour of death and the accounting which I must then render of time ill-spent, of talents unemployed, of good undone, and of my empty pride in success, which is so fatal to the work of God.

All for Jesus, all through Mary, all in imitation of thee, O Patriarch Joseph! This shall be my watchword in life and in death. Amen.

St. Joseph, Model of Workmen, pray for us!

St. Joseph, Most Faithful

"Of whom the world was not worthy; wandering in deserts, in mountains, and in dens, and in caves of the earth. And all these being approved by the testimony of faith, received not the promise."

—Hebrews 11:38–39

In the Epistle to the Hebrews, St. Paul relates the stories of faith of the patriarchs and matriarchs of the past. He gives us a definition of faith in the first verse of the chapter: "Now faith is the substance of things to be hoped for, the evidence of things that appear not." To say that faith is a substance is to say that it is a real thing, the sum of particular parts that make up a whole.[18] Faith is not simply an

---

18 Faith has both an objective and subjective meaning. Although they are related, they mean slightly different things. Objectively, the Faith is the sum of all the truths revealed by God that the Church teaches *De Fide*. Subjectively, faith stands for the virtue (habit) by which we assent to those truths. Moreover, an act of faith is related both to the object of the intellect and the object of the will. If you think of the simple prayer the *Act of Faith* that forms part of our daily morning prayer, you'll have a good understanding of what faith is. For a more comprehensive treatment of faith in all its meanings and dimensions, you can study St. Thomas Aquinas's

ethereal and amorphous abstraction as many would have us believe. To have faith is not merely to hope; hence, Paul says it is the substance of things hoped for and not simply the act of hoping.

When a man has faith, he is in possession of something invaluable, something that acts as an impenetrable bulwark against life's suffering and trials. Faith is not only an intellectual reality but should be a habitual disposition of your soul, one might even say the fixed orientation of a man's whole being toward God.[19] Our intellect is contained in our soul, and thus we could say that what we believe affects— even changes—who we are. Since our intellect is in our soul and our soul is the form of our body, our credence for or against a specific idea has the potential to alter everything about us.

Simply put, what we know to be true in the depths of our being is the "stuff" we are made of. Think of a man of true faith whom you've encountered. Men like this are constructed from something otherworldly; they don't live by the same norms, maxims, and values most commonly found among men. They have a resolve that defies what most consider reasonable. No matter the era or circumstance, a man of true faith lives with his compass directed toward God,

---

Summa Theologiae. The first seven questions of the Second Part of the Second Part deal with faith.

19 Faith is a supernatural gift that God infuses into man at Baptism. Since it is supernatural, men cannot create faith, acquire it on their own, or give it to someone else, though men can serve as instruments used by God to bring others to the Faith. One who is baptized does not lose this gift of faith unless he commits a sin against the Faith, such as heresy (or apostasy). In this, it differs from the supernatural gift of charity, which is lost with any one mortal sin.

overcoming any and all obstacles. What makes faith such a mystery to the skeptic is that a man can be so certain of the truth of the matter, even when that thing is yet to be seen.

Imagine for a moment St. Joseph after the visitation of the Archangel Gabriel. St. Joseph did not doubt in the classic sense regarding the chastity of the Blessed Mother. No, he understood quite well what the angel had to say. Through eyes and ears of faith, St. Joseph understood to his very core, without hesitation, that the coming of the long-awaited Messiah was at hand. There is good reason to believe that St. Joseph even knew of the coming Crucifixion and that he would not be able to be there to protect his wife and Son. In Catholic devotion, this is referred to as the passion of St. Joseph.

To suggest that St. Joseph went through a passion of his own is to say that he suffered a great deal, especially throughout his dying moments. Regardless of the physical dimensions of that suffering, what is important to consider is the interior suffering experienced by St. Joseph. His foreknowledge of the death of his divine Son was hard enough to bear, but the thought of being absent at that crucial time was even worse.

Every father knows that the greatest fear we have is failing to protect and provide for our families. I am sure fathers can relate to the anxious feeling of lying awake at night, hearing a noise from somewhere in the house, and then immediately contemplating a plan of action to protect loved ones from violence. In addition, fathers today have to contend with the innumerable threats that lie in wait for our children in the spiritual and moral sphere. What will be on TV at their cousin's home? Will someone on the school

bus show them evil images on a smart phone? What leer-
ing looks or vulgar comments might their daughters face?
What bullying or peer pressure toward evil will they be
subjected to? What anti-Catholic garbage might they hear
in a world gone mad?

In many such situations, fathers will not be able to be
present to protect their families. Needless to say, as fathers,
we cannot do what we are required to do for our families on
our own. Therefore, we must rely on the spiritual weapons
available to us as powerful defenses as well as our own
guardian angels and those angels assigned by God to watch
over the members of our families. To raise a child today as
a faithful Catholic takes a commensurate level of faith: the
more severe the danger, the greater the faith that is required.

St. Joseph could see in his soul what was to befall his
Son. He saw the nails; he felt the rippling inertia emanating
forth from each infinitely dense drop of Precious Blood as
it hit the ground. He saw in Mary's face a tragic countenance, a sorrowful consolation as her immaculate beauty
reflected the Crucifixion as a culmination of the Annunciation. St. Joseph took his dying breaths knowing that in a
moment he could say "it is finished" as he prepared to give
up the ghost.

Most importantly, St. Joseph knew that death was not the
end and that his forthcoming resting place in the Limbo of
the Fathers would be a springboard to heavenly glory. He
had faith in the Resurrection.[20] Surrounded by patriarchs

---

20 St. Paul explains that without the Resurrection, our faith is useless.
    He writes, "Now if Christ be preached, that he arose again from the
    dead, how do some among you say, that there is no resurrection of
    the dead? But if there be no resurrection of the dead, then Christ is

in Abraham's bosom, he continued in unmatchable faith, awaiting that moment of reunification with Jesus, to whom he could once again say in union with God the Father, "This is my beloved Son, in whom I am well pleased."

St. Joseph, Most Faithful, pray for us!

St. Joseph, Protector of the Church

Our Father in faith, St. Joseph, raised Our Lord for the first portion of his life in Egypt, a nation under the dominion of demons and idols. He protected Jesus Christ and the Mother of God on their journeys across unforgiving and hostile deserts. What a perfect example to which we can turn during these hard times.

Who cannot see that our society is now like a theater of war? In every form of media, we see the enemy on the offensive. Our schools and public institutions have been co-opted and are used to subvert our own children. Addictive technology and chemical substances are used to enslave many. Landmines of demonic influence are set everywhere to trap unwitting souls in hidden places. The enemy has even infiltrated the holy sanctuary with his agents, and the smoke of Satan has entered the very temple of God.

The expression of true Christian devotion in public places can today bring upon faithful men and women the scorn and castigation of their peers and government officials. As hard as this epoch may seem, we have been created by God for exactly this moment, and he will provide the requisite graces to persevere if we properly dispose ourselves.

---

not risen again. And if Christ be not risen again, then is our preaching vain, and your faith is also vain" (1 Cor. 15:12–14).

The ultimate invasion of Christendom is an invasion by the spirit of antichrist, and we must rely on St. Joseph, Protector of the Church, to be our holy general against the forces of hell. From the day of Christ's birth to the day of St. Joseph's death, the holy patriarch lived a life in firm resistance to the wiles of the demons who sought to harm his Son. This holy man of renown protected Jesus Christ and the Mother of God in both the physical and spiritual sense. He did this through his humility, his fortitude, his devotion, and love of God. The life of St. Joseph was a living, breathing sermon on spiritual warfare, a blueprint for holy resistance against malice.

Like St. Joseph, many of the Crusaders died in battle, not yet reaching the Holy Land, just as Joseph died before the Resurrection. These ancestors of ours gave their lives, swinging their swords under the banner of Our Lord, fueled by love of Holy Mother Church and an insatiable yearning to pass on to their progeny the holy things that were given to them. Against all odds, they did great things, and we can be certain that with St. Joseph in heaven, thousands of these unnamed saints intercede for us with the ferocity of soldiers enlisted in the heavenly host.

We have inherited a great responsibility, too great for us to bear alone. For this reason, we must turn to St. Joseph as Protector of the Church and seek to conform our will to God's in the way that he did. Our spouses, our children, and our Church depend on just men to rise up once again and march against the gates of hell. At times, we may encounter seeming defeat, and it may even appear as if all hope is lost. But we are in possession of a power that the enemy does not have: the power of the Resurrection. Never allow yourself to forget that "the Lord himself shall come down from heaven with commandment, and with the voice of an archangel, and with the trumpet of God: and the dead who are in Christ, shall rise first" (1 Thess. 4:15).

St. Joseph, Protector of the Church, pray for us!

St. Joseph, Terror of Demons

The Angel Gabriel brought the message of the Incarnation to the Blessed Mother. The name Gabriel in Hebrew means two things: "strength of God" and "man of God." It is no accident that the man of God came to announce to Mary the coming God-man. Furthermore, according to Cornelius à Lapide, SJ (d. 1637), Gabriel oversees the conflicts of the faithful, hence his carrying of God's strength.

Gabriel announced the Incarnation, but in doing so, he announced war. The heavenly conflict between Michael and Lucifer would now take place on the soil of earth, and God's Son would enter the battle under the guise of an infant. With her *fiat*, the Immaculate Virgin proclaimed to heaven and hell that the battle for souls was in its decisive stage. The theater of war between the angels and the demons would find itself in the womb of the Blessed Virgin. St. Joseph was called to guard this woman, and because of this, he was sent forth by God to terrorize the devils who sought to foil the divine plan.

For years, Joseph spent hours perfecting his craft, striving and sweating in his workshop. Like a foreshadowing of the new Adam, Joseph worked by the sweat of his brow, taming the dried flesh of the trees of the Holy Land. In the manner that God whittles down a man, transforming him from a rough plank to a man perfected, so too did Joseph bend and form the elements that would become the cross of his adopted Son. The demons are never truly absent, even at our hour of death; thus, with each passing year, the devils assigned by hell to tempt Joseph watched him ever so closely. They watched as Joseph, regenerated in his mother's womb, grew in chastity and manliness.

"There is something different about him," the demons thought. His perfected countenance and temperate demeanor confused the devils. How could a man so humble also demonstrate the fortitude of a dragon slayer? From the shadows, they observed Joseph chop down trees and prepare them for transport. Like a painful instance of sanctified déjà vu, these demons saw a flash of the Christ as St. Joseph knelt to the ground, only to stand with a tree on his shoulders. Watching the Terror of Demons carry oak and olive trees was torturous. The evil spirits were paralyzed and incompetent while Joseph taunted them with an image of the coming *via dolorosa*, forced to seethe with impotent rage at the eternal advent. As Joseph lifted his hammer to pound iron, each metallic clang smashed the gates of hell like the cheerful piercing of the bells of consecration.

Soon enough, Jesus Christ would apprentice his earthly father in his workshop. The entrance of the Son of Man into Joseph's domain transformed this humble space into a foundry of divine grace. The demons, bound by their own self-hatred, were forced to watch as Christ sanctified the implements of his crucifixion, like he sanctified the waters of baptism. The years Christ spent under the tutelage of his adoptive father only added to the pain of hell. The Terror of Demons guided the hands of the Child of Mary as they taunted the fallen angels with their unconditional love. Unyielding labor, the curse of Adam, had been reversed and turned into the playground of messianic mirth. We might even imagine Christ, as a young man, pricking his finger on a sharpened tool. Out of his sacred hand dripped the precious blood, hydrating the fallen world, ever thirsting for the Crucifixion.

Of all the men ever born, it was Joseph, born of the line of David, whom God chose for this sacred duty. The holiness of St. Joseph makes him a terror to those who seek to terrorize the souls of men. He taunted the tempters and made holy mockery of the fallen angels. May we seek to imitate him in our pursuit of sanctity and beg that the divine craftsman may whittle away at our sinful inclinations.

Every man will find himself in situations that he cannot overcome by his natural powers alone. This is because his battle is with preternatural powers whose nature far exceeds his own ability, tenacity, and intelligence. To fulfill his duty of protecting his family and guiding his family along the path marked by Christ, he absolutely requires supernatural aid. In such situations, husbands and fathers must call on heavenly aid.

Have frequent recourse to Our Lady, to St. Michael, to your guardian angel, to your patron saint, and never forget to also turn to St. Joseph. He has great authority and power over these preternatural powers and, by his assistance, we too can become terrors for the devils.

St. Joseph, Terror of Demons, pray for us!

Placeat tibi, Sancta Trinitas.